RUDOLF KEMPE
Pictures of a Life

RUDOLF KEMPE
Pictures of a Life

Preface by Dietrich Fischer-Dieskau
Compilation and text by Cordula Kempe-Oettinger
Picture Consultant: Werner Neumeister

SPRINGWOOD BOOKS

First published 1977 by Paul List Verlag KG, Munich
English translation © Cordula Kempe-Oettinger 1979

All rights reserved. No part of this publication may be reproduced, stored in a retrieval system, or transmitted, in any form or by any means, electronic, mechanical, photocopying, recording or otherwise, without the prior permission of Springwood Books Ltd., 49/51 Bedford Row, London

Printed in Great Britain by Butler and Tanner Ltd.
Frome and London

ISBN 0 9059 4706 1

Contents

Preface by Dietrich Fischer-Dieskau	7
Foreword	10
Rudi Kempe—Oboist	14
Towards the Conductor's Desk	20
Post-War Years: an End and a Beginning	29
Picture Section: 1912–1954	37
'Jet Set'	55
Picture Section: 1955–1969	63
Man and Musician	101
Picture Section: 1970–1976	121
Discography	162
Acknowledgements	180
Illustration Acknowledgements	180

Preface

Rudolf Kempe was one of the very small group of German conductors who during the last decades enjoyed an international reputation. Yet one cannot understand his individuality in terms of the exclusiveness inherent in the still prevalent idea of the 'German' conductor, or indeed of any nationalist label (as if these concepts had not lost all real significance today). Those listeners and musicians who might want to label him in such a way do not know that Kempe, during his all-too-short working life, showed how much he disliked the narrowness and specialisation that such definitions imply.

This is not to deny his roots in Germany, which, in the nineteenth century, could with some justification be called the Mecca of music. He started his career in Leipzig, which since Mendelssohn's day had been one of Europe's great centres of music. The young Kempe, both oboist and pianist, had many contacts with Karl Straube, then cantor of St. Thomas's Church. The Gewandhaus and Neues Theater were his artistic homes.

An artist of Kempe's quality was deeply aware of musical traditions and grieved to see them in jeopardy. Only in the orchestras can be found traces of the formerly distinctive national styles of playing in both string and wind techniques. They are dying out in favour of the perfection of uniformity that leads to such anonymous effects in the concert hall and from loudspeakers. Kempe, himself closely familiar with the style of many different orchestras, served a nobler ideal. He, who regarded artistic ability as a given precondition for musical existence, had at heart the preservation of artistic values. He took this to mean the bringing to life of the printed note, the obtaining of an infinite variety of subtleties, the ability to surprise himself and his audience again and again and thus never to let interest flag. That one cannot take such things for granted is obvious when one looks at what usually happens in front of and in the orchestra.

Kempe successfully avoided what seems increasingly to be a danger today: exaggeration for the sake of effect on the one hand, and stiffness as a result of seeking clinical perfection on the other. Only a chosen few, such as Kempe, can realise their intentions by re-creating and at the same time remaining true to the original.

Rudolf Kempe should not only be remembered as an interpreter of his particular favourites, Schumann, Brahms, Wagner or Strauss. Can we expect to hear again such interpretations—lucid, not merely idiomatic—of works by Dvořák, Tchaikovsky, Shostakovich or Bartók?

One characteristic, possessed by only a few conductors, distinguished Kempe: his modesty. While we were rehearsing together for some performances and a recording of the Brahms German Requiem he said something which I still remember vividly, because it moved me deeply: 'If only I could conduct this half as beautifully as Furtwängler did in Vienna the other day, I'd be happy.' And then followed a performance which, while in some ways resembling Furtwängler's, bore his personal stamp in every detail.

The magic in all his interpretations was shared by listeners in America as well as by those in England or Switzerland. His graceful virtuoso stick technique was in no way typical of that which one normally associates with the German Kapellmeister; neither heavy nor stiff, with no severe sense of mission, neither scourge-like nor laden with priestly dedication, it conveyed rather the impression of an effortless fusion of music, orchestra and audience.

When I first met him in 1950, we were both travelling to Vienna to make our débuts there, but in different venues. He had to conduct *Meistersinger* at the State Opera the next evening and was hoping for an ensemble rehearsal the same morning. As it happened to be a Sunday, no one turned up, and in the evening he had to face a cast utterly unknown to him. Nevertheless, the performance showed the typical results of his stick technique: transparency, unobtrusiveness, and an especially great attention to the limits of his singers' powers of projection.

Enjoyment through play was one of his life's maxims, and this meant not only in his leisure time, when he would build his model railways. This last pleasure could be happily indulged, since the use of his hands was basic to his profession.

When, as happened in our *Lohengrin* recording, through the hysteria of a few of the singers and some sudden but unavoidable cast changes, everything seemed to go haywire, he stood there like a rock, quiet and kind, amid the waves of excitement.

Kempe was a man of few words. Towards the end of his life, however, he felt the urge to put down on paper his experiences and insights, and also to hand them down through teaching. He found himself at odds with, and profoundly disturbed by, the dangerous development in the training of musicians and orchestras, especially by the lack of an organic education for the young, quite apart from the nadir in creative production. His notes, irreversibly interrupted before they could be brought into a finished form, contain invaluable material for young musicians. This book tries to draw a picture of his life and work. May its many readers continue to benefit from his example and memory.

Dietrich Fischer-Dieskau
May 1977

Foreword

All his life Rudolf Kempe shunned publicity—through natural shyness, and through a sense of responsibility as an interpreter which precluded pretentiousness and egotism. When he decided to have the experiences of his musical life published in the form of a biography (still to be completed), he did so reluctantly, and only after considerable deliberation. As a formative incident, his contribution to the book *Great Interpreters in Conversation* prompted him to abandon the reserve he had maintained throughout his life; for the first time he forced himself to make known in writing his thoughts about music. This was a contradiction not only for Kempe the man and the musician but probably for music itself. Indeed it was this very contradiction which seemed to pinpoint for him the present crisis in music and in basic human concerns. Nowadays, when the commercialism of the media is debasing the spirit of art by idle chatter, some creative and performing artists have been driven into an attitude of passive resignation because they are neither able nor willing to compromise their own nature and the nature of their art. How far such an attitude of withdrawal on the part of those seriously concerned was responsible for the development of false values was a question which troubled Rudolf Kempe more than he cared to admit. The devaluation of musical ideals, far more frightening than any material devaluation because it cannot be measured in statistical terms—this could not but depress a man like him. As a result his cheerful nature sometimes was darkened by clouds which hung over his work. 'I often long just to sit at home making music only for myself.'

With good reason many young and insecure musicians would seek his advice and help. But Kempe had realised long before that it was not sufficient to give conducting lessons to a handful of talented students, particularly because 'Conducting does not belong to the things that can be taught. It can only be learnt with experience.' In addition, the ability to translate musical feeling immediately into meaningful gestures was regarded by him as an essential precondition, innate and not to be explained. Yet his own experience urged him to pass on the results of a lifetime's work. To young musicians, who nowadays hardly see a chance of developing organically, he endeavoured to show how to make the most of their natural talents. By describing his own course as a conductor, he tried to support and encourage those who were ready to progress, like him, in an undemonstrative way. It was not his intention to litter the booksellers' shelves with yet another book of self-adulatory comments. This may be obvious to all who knew Kempe's unpretentious music-making; they may have appreciated something of his nature from the way he made them appreciate the nature of music.

This picture book is intended for these people, not only because it will take some years to finish the autobiography he left in draft, but for another reason. Rudolf Kempe's ability to elicit the form and essence of music from his instrument, the orchestra—to which he would hardly talk—manifested itself merely through his gestures with a directness and concentration unusual even among conductors. This was apparent the very moment he came in contact with musicians. Photographs capturing such moments may complement visually what is otherwise presented only by radio and gramophone recordings. They recapture the spontaneity of original interpretations and thus enable us to re-experience what happens on the threshold between the comprehensible and the incomprehensible. How that moment is created by mental and physical forces alike, how it unites different individuals, in concert, rehearsal or even recording session, how it alternates between tension and relaxation—all this may be of interest to listeners and to performers.

The present selection of photographs covers a period of more than sixty years, and represents in its way a small history of photographic art—a fact that explains why some reproductions are of a lesser quality than others. However, some technical flaws may be outweighed by a picture's content or expression. Some of the photos were taken by Rudolf Kempe himself and these may indicate a side of his character quite surprising in a musician. He was a man who experienced as much through his eyes as his ears. His way from orchestral desk to conductor's podium was made possible not least by his power of observation. And an important counterpart to his music was his intense involvement with the visual. Whatever revealed itself to him through his eyes was stored up and later drawn on as a source of feeling and inspiration. In filming and photography he found an outlet for his own creativity—something in music he never dared to attempt. 'To compose? No, this I leave to others. I fear I've nothing to say except rubbish.' And with a soft smile which began in the eyes he would put the subject aside. His Saxon dialect, which he never entirely lost, returned at such moments and was a sign of understatement characteristically his. Whenever he felt deeply about something he would react nonchalantly—if at all.

By peering through a microscope or telescope he tried to place himself and his work in a more truthful context, and find momentary escape from the dogmatic values he questioned. Absorbed in the view of a dewdrop or galaxy, he found confirmation of his own belief how little it matters to put materialistic labels on anything. Somehow he accepted man's basic insecurity, and in so doing found security in himself—a security that allowed others to feel secure with him. Therefore what is perhaps the most dangerous temptation for any conductor, to win and abuse power over others, was something Rudolf Kempe never knew. His destiny was to be that of a performing servant, and he accepted it without question. Never demanding more, never giving less, he followed this destiny with a simplicity deep in his heart which was his true strength. As an interpreter he guarded without wishing to possess, and he held in his hands—hands that could unravel and set right all sorts of confusion with indescribable tenderness—something which had been entrusted to him: a slender thread that links man with his maker.

Perhaps he was even unaware of this himself.

Rudi Kempe—Oboist

One thing is certain: from generation to generation the Kempe family had been totally unmusical.

No one would ever have imagined that Rudi, an unassuming, well-behaved child, was destined to be different from his ancestors—until one day when he was just tall enough to reach an old piece of furniture that had been left somewhere in his parent's house, an inn called *Zur Guten Quelle* (The Good Spring). God knows how it got there, and that it still had keys was amazing. Yet it is unlikely that anyone would ever have taken notice of it, had not this little boy begun to show his liking for the unusual piece of furniture—to the annoyance of the people around him.

Their annoyance finally resulted in a family council being called and a teacher being found to discipline the boy's wild attacks on the keyboard. Later, when he was eight years old and when the piano alone could not satisfy his insatiable thirst for music-making, the boy turned his attention to an old fiddle which had seen better days. This fully occupied him until he was thirteen. Then, by chance, his grown-up cousin Hilde turned up; her intuition induced her to take the boy to an opera performance.

This was given in Gottfried Semper's Opera House in Dresden, said by many to have been the most beautiful opera house in the world. The orchestra of the Dresden Staatskapelle, regarded by Wagner as 'the miraculous harp', was playing. The opera was Mozart's *Magic Flute*. The little boy, born in the village of Niederpoyritz on the outskirts of Dresden and brought up in an ordinary inn, for the first time in his life heard an orchestra playing the music of Mozart. 'I only know that never before and perhaps never since has any sound thrilled me as did the E♭ chord at the opening of the *Magic Flute* overture.'

The Kempes were unaware of the significance of this event. Rudi was a bright boy and was admitted as a pupil to the Tradesman's High School in Dresden. It was Easter 1924 and he began to battle with mathematics, book-keeping and other commercial subjects which, in the eyes of his parents, were—unlike music—essential. The way he knuckled down to these studies—at least for the time being—pleased everybody. However, the event once again shows what happens when honest people like the Kempes do what they feel is right and leave the rest to God. By coincidence the fourth floor of the Tradesman's High School building temporarily housed the recently founded Orchestral School of the Dresden Staatskapelle.

By this time Rudi had worn out several piano teachers: 'Mother, I'm not going to stay any longer with that woman! Why, she doesn't even know when I'm playing wrong notes!' Now this seemingly demanding boy, with his inborn quiet persistence, managed to persuade his mother to climb up to that fourth floor 'just to see what it's like there....' They found a number of Orchestral School teachers, all of them principals of the Dresden Staatskapelle, who began to examine the fourteen-year-old boy in piano and violin playing and in exacting aural tests. 'The violin playing was barely average,' recalled the candidate. 'The piano playing went better, and so did the aural tests.' Of course, one has to understand what it meant when he said 'went better'. The examiners were astounded by what they had heard, yet no one there could have foreseen that one day some of them would play under the direction of this young boy and, what is more, enjoy doing so. They unanimously agreed that 'Rudi Kempe must stay here', so parental resistance and family objections were defeated; Rudi began the full-time study of music.

Straight away he was put through the mill with piano, violin, chamber music and theory classes, but after a while it became clear that his musical capacities were not being stretched. Since the school orchestra was short of woodwind players, notably oboists, it was decided—after a brief examination of his physical aptitude—that Rudi should study the oboe as well. Up to this time, the boy hardly knew of the existence of this instrument. Now, by dint of gentle patience (part of his nature and also a Saxon characteristic—'just wait and see'), he took to the oboe and began lessons with Johannes König.

This impressive man, principal oboist of the Dresden Staatskapelle and a highly respected teacher of several generations of fine musicians, did much more than guide the boy's musical instruction. Whenever Rudi's father shook his head in despair— 'I can't think what those little fingers are doing'—then Johannes König came to the rescue and like a guardian took decisions on his pupil's behalf. König's teaching method was based on the aims and ideals set out by Fritz Busch, who had founded the Orchestral School of the Dresden Staatskapelle, known as the O.S.K. During their studies, talented pupils were made familiar with all technical and musical problems, not least those of coping with the everyday life of being an orchestral player. Leading instrumentalists of a first-rate orchestra, with nearly four centuries of tradition to uphold, offered solutions to these problems—solutions that are not always obvious from reading scores or books on theory. Above all, in the Dresden Staatskapelle, there was no question of a 'deputy system'. Teachers did not regard their pupils merely as substitutes for themselves whenever they wanted to escape routine opera performances. 'Gradually they made us grow into the orchestra and worked the miracle that whenever we pupils were permitted to play with the orchestra, its playing did not fall to a "deputy" standard. On the contrary, the so-called deputies somehow managed to reach the standards of the Dresden Staatskapelle. Apart from instrumental instruction our teachers made us realise what music is all about. We learnt how to enjoy music-making and at the same time how to be self-disciplined, appreciating the achievement of others. They made us aware how important it is to depend and rely on one another for any kind of ensemble playing, and to respect what it means to be a member of a professional orchestra.' Whenever Rudolf Kempe recalled his teachers he regretted that their outlook and attitude hardly exist nowadays. To be an orchestral musician is today to belong to a respected profession; but even so and with much improved remuneration, the idealism of players sometimes lasts no longer than their first season.

Rudi Kempe in those days had not the slightest idea of the profession he had chosen, or rather which had chosen him. Apart from his cousin Hilde, no one in the family had ever been tempted to approach music, least of all the classics. So he entered a new world, a world that was unquestionably and unaccountably his own. He found himself alone, without family support or encouragement, but also free from any obligation to keep up a family tradition. That he fell into hands like those of his teachers in Dresden was more than good fortune—it was almost destiny. Thanks to them, an important part of his nature was revealed and developed which in later years, when he was a conductor, was to distinguish him from others: his ability to see himself as 'primus inter pares'.

Admittedly, Kempe's was a strict training. It is not surprising that the tall and lanky youth needed the twelve pieces of plum cake which he effortlessly managed to gulp down with two cups of cocoa in a cheap café to sustain himself during the day. The strains of the student's life were not lessened by his parents' opinion: 'You've got yourself into it, so you'd better get yourself out of it.' The *Gute Quelle* in Dresden-Blasewitz was still a good spring when it came to keeping a roof over his head and putting something in his stomach—but when it came to luxuries like money for lessons or music, he found that the spring dried up. However, poverty has never been a setback to talented people, and it was not to Rudi Kempe—on the contrary. What he learnt during the relatively short period of his four years of studies, he had to turn to practical advantage right away: in order to make ends meet he played in cinemas, churches and coffee shops. But he soon discovered that in these surroundings the violin was not for him the best of instruments. 'My intonation was lousy, and to improve it I would have needed to practise endlessly.' At least he had mastered Kreutzer's studies and those highly regarded but much hated concertos by Seitz.

The piano on the other hand offered greater scope. Thanks to a remarkable technique and an outstanding ability to sight read, he acquired all kinds of repertoire, absorbing like a sponge everything from Bach to ragtime. Before long his versatility became known, and he was regularly invited to play in all kinds of places, travelling with his friends and colleagues along the River Elbe—on foot, by bike or occasionally in luxury by train or steam boat—from Dresden far into Sächsische Schweiz. A friend, Erich Donnerhack (later to become head of light music at Leipzig Radio), had discovered a café in the lovely village of Bad Schandau where every weekend he entertained at the piano the tourists who visited the place from all round. The proprietress was anxious to add some tone to her establishment, and Erich—who not only preferred the violin to the piano but actually played it better—persuaded her that someone else should join him as pianist. His friend Rudi was appointed to accompany him, and one Saturday afternoon the pair made their way to Bad Schandau to find on the café door an enormous poster announcing: 'Today—Augmented Orchestra—Kapelle Donnerhack.' The two-piece Kapelle Donnerhack, whose paltry fee did not even justify the purchase of suitable music, treated the audience to a series of improvised arrangements of studies and concert pieces from their O.S.K. classes—given as tea-sipping music from two in the afternoon until eight, and as clod-hopping dance music from eight until two o'clock in the morning. Generous supplies of beer and (on rare occasions) liqueurs had to be hidden in the piano itself in the time-honoured way, in order to save the two musicians, the following day, from falling off their seats when attending theory lessons at the O.S.K. or playing in a Bach Cantata rehearsal in the Martin Luther Kirche.

These escapades apart, Rudi was making such rapid progress with the oboe that after only four years of study his mentor Johannes König nominated him, without Rudi knowing, to audition as first oboe in the Dortmund Orchestra, where a vacancy had occurred. 'Just you go there, young man, and play. Then you'll find out what it is like to audition.' Rudi in fact had no idea what it was like, but journeyed to Dortmund and got the job.

Undoubtedly König knew what he was doing. On various occasions he had tested

ORCHESTERSCHULE
DER
SÄCHSISCHEN STAATSKAPELLE e. V.

Abschlußprüfungen
des Winter-Semesters 1927/28

2. Prüfungs-Konzert

Montag, den 30. Januar 1928, abends ½8 Uhr, Dresdner Kaufmannschaft

1. **Joh. Seb. Bach:** Konzert in D-moll für 2 Violinen mit Orchester
   Vivace — Largo ma non tanto — Allegro
   Bruno Knauer (Klasse Kam.-Mus. Krüger)
   Rosa Müller (Klasse Kam.-Virt. Lederer)

2. **E. Wolf-Ferrari:** Opus 8, Kammer-Sinfonie für Pianoforte, 2 Violinen, Viola, Violoncello, Contrabaß, Flöte, Oboe, Klarinette, Fagott und Horn
   Allegro moderato — Adagio — Vivace con spirito — Finale
   Schmidt, Roth, Muck, Fellmer, Eva Wille, Mathé, Piperow, Kempe, Zschiedrich, Arnold, Rhode

3. **Friedebald Gräfe:** Konzertino B-dur für Posaune und Orchester
   Alfons Orpky (Klasse Kam.-Virt. Arnold)

4. **Fr. Liszt:** 2. Konzert A-dur
   Helmut Schaefer (Klasse Karl Fehling)

Leitung des Schüler-Orchesters:
Prof. Georg Wille

Konzertflügel: Julius Blüthner, aus dem Magazin Dresden-A., Prager Straße 12

Der Reinertrag aus dem Programm-Verkauf fließt dem
Freistellen-Fonds zu!

his star pupil (everyone recognised he was—except Rudi himself), steering him through concerts with the O.S.K., or with a 'town and gown' orchestra, and allowing him to perform professionally at the Martin Luther Kirche and in chamber-music evenings with his teachers—Karl Schütte, Fritz Rucker and König himself. It seemed the most natural thing in the world that Rudi should play as a member of his teachers' ensemble, and as a result he overcame his natural shyness and stage fright.

With a solid musical groundwork given him by his teachers and the mysterious farewell advice of his taciturn father spoken on Dresden railway station, 'Be careful you don't fall ill', the eighteen-year-old Rudi suddenly found himself standing on his own feet. Life began. 'Life' meant the loneliness of a rented room and his work with the Dortmund Orchestra, which was not very exciting. It lasted four months. Then he received a telegram from Johannes König commanding him to go to Leipzig to audition for the post of principal oboe in the Gewandhaus Orchestra. There were forty-four other candidates. 'Every one of them seemed better than the last, and I thought it was a crazy notion that I should play there.' It took three days for the Gewandhaus committee to hear the forty-five oboists. Rudi Kempe was appointed.

The Gewandhaus Orchestra, like the Dresden Staatskapelle, served both as symphony and opera orchestra and the newly appointed first oboe was considerably taxed. Alternating with an older colleague, Alfred Gleissberg, he had to perform between concerts in no less than fourteen different operas within four weeks: *The Mikado, Butterfly, Carmen, Così fan tutte, Tosca, Rigoletto, Mignon, Si j'étais Roi, Zar und Zimmermann, Rienzi, Eugene Onegin, The Barber of Baghdad, Undine* and *Parsifal*. Apart from the physical demands, it was not easy for a beginner to sight read in performance works which contain solo passages often feared even by players with years of experience. Playing at sight was a risky necessity. However, the skill given him by Johannes König, the many evenings spent in the gallery and the orchestra pit of the Dresden Opera House, together with the countless scores he had devoured, now paid off. Supported by the loyalty of his more experienced colleagues, Rudi Kempe apparently succeeded, and did not disgrace his teachers, the Gewandhaus or himself.

Towards the Conductor's Desk

'The good thing about Leipzig was that it was not as far from Dresden as Dortmund.' So Rudi's connections with home were kept alive. First at the *Gute Quelle*, where the Kapelle Donnerhack, now enlarged to mammoth proportions by their friend and oboist Herbert Karger, turned up whenever the trio were hungry. Secondly the connection with Johannes König grew stronger. The former pupil, now a colleague at the rival Gewandhaus, was by this time on Christian-name terms with his teacher. König would take him and some friends on holiday to the Allgäu Alps, chasing them up and down the mountains to make the youngsters forget the strains of musical life. Exchanging white tie and tails for *lederhosen* and climbing boots, and replacing the oboe with a cigar, König let his pupils into the secret of 'philosophising about nothing'—an art which is peculiar to the Saxons.

The ability to switch off was in fact one of Rudi Kempe's characteristics, and in this he was encouraged not least by his old teacher. Johannes König had learnt from the experience of a lifetime that the power of concentration, which enables an artist to give of his best, depends mainly on his capacity to relax.

Incidentally it was König who once during a lesson had remarked, 'Rudi, I think one day you will become a conductor. You've got the cut for it!' All those who had heard this had burst out laughing, including Rudi himself. No one knew better than König that it was not the 'cut'.... However, his well-intended forecast 'No, dear boy, you'll not remain an oboist for long!' did not stir up any ambition to become a conductor in the boy's mind. The fact that Rudi during his Dresden student days, and while he was with the Gewandhaus Orchestra, would follow everything in full score (he kept a copy by his side during rehearsals and performances) had nothing to do with König's forecast. He simply felt the need to engross himself in music. He knew he could only play his part in an orchestral work to his own satisfaction if he had studied the score and knew the entire context. In this way he came to know precisely what his colleagues had to do at any given moment, and to listen to the way they were playing their parts. Accordingly he could regulate his dynamics in solo and tutti sections alike, alter his colouring and adjust his own nuances in tempo, 'nuances which in earlier days were not only permitted but expected!' This basic concept of chamber music that can be—and should be—applied to any ensemble playing was one of his strengths; not only had he learnt it, it was part of his nature.

It was only to be expected, therefore, that chamber music would play an important part in his life, notwithstanding the busy schedule of the Leipzig opera and the Gewandhaus—a schedule far more taxing than is the case in Germany nowadays. It did not take long for his colleagues to elect the twenty-one-year-old 'Kammervirtuoso' (a title not normally bestowed on players at this early age) to a position in the Gewandhaus wind quintet. He was to play with them for many years. That he was a versatile pianist was also soon discovered in Leipzig, as it had been in Dresden. There was hardly an orchestral colleague or singer who would not ask him to accompany them as a 'maid of all work'. He would play anything anywhere, whether in distinguished recitals in the Gewandhaus or Conservatoire or at social events at various clubs which were greedy for culture. The latter occasions were more profit-

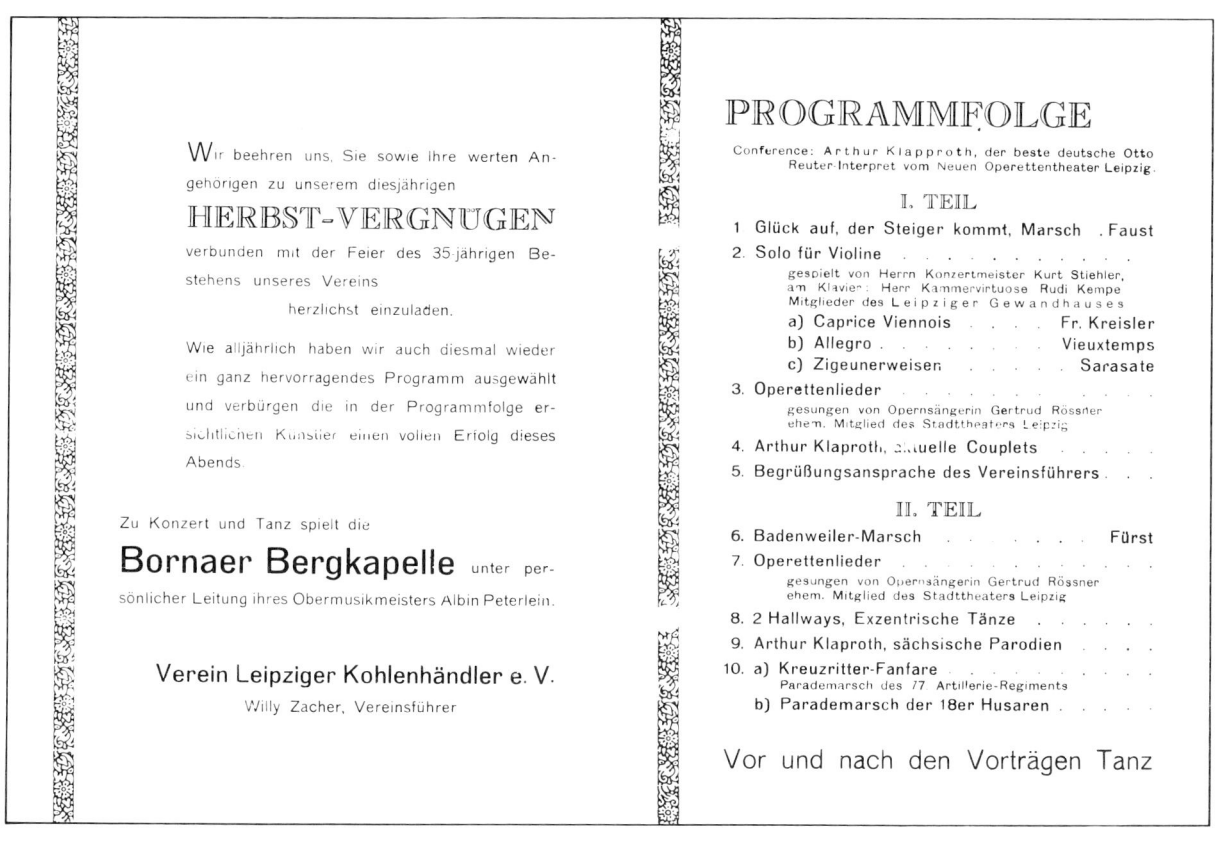

able, of course, though less so for the accompanist. Kempe once played an entire programme for the Leipzig Coal Merchants Society accompanying his friend, the Gewandhaus leader Kurt Stiehler, and a group of singers and dancers from the Leipzig Opera; each of them was paid a princely fee of 100 marks. Kempe's fee consisted of a handshake from the Chairman, who with the words 'You did all right, lad', thrust a five-mark piece into his palm. This is typical of the musical world's age-old attitude towards the 'man at the keyboard'—an attitude occasionally displayed even towards artists like Gerald Moore. And it is also typical of Rudi Kempe's life. He never became a businessman. Clearly he had left the Tradesman's High School too early. But he did not care; by hard work and saving, he managed slowly but surely to fulfil his most ardent desire: he bought a grand piano—secondhand of course. He appeared to live on music alone.

At that time the Leipzig opera was led by a pupil of Gustav Mahler named Gustav Brecher. As chief conductor Brecher had set an unusually high standard of opera performance due to his thorough rehearsal techniques; for a repertory piece like *Fra Diavolo* he would expect six orchestral rehearsals alone. Likewise on the concert stage the Gewandhaus Orchestra had become a musical centre for conductors, famous then and since, conductors who were highly regarded and whose reputations were based on their ability. There were regular visiting guests like Fritz Busch from neighbouring Dresden, Erich Kleiber, Otto Klemperer, Carl Schuricht, Thomas Beecham and Clemens Krauss. Of particular importance were Bruno Walter and Wilhelm Furtwängler, the latter being Artur Nikisch's successor and Walter's predecessor as chief conductor of the Gewandhaus. They influenced to a high degree the Leipzig music scene, and consequently influenced the young Rudi Kempe. From his oboe desk he would observe every move of their stick technique and expression, noting contrasting methods and judging reactions between conductor and instrumentalists in the closest detail. No matter whether it was the broad flamboyant gestures of Furtwängler or the spare, almost dry baton technique of Richard Strauss; what was decisive was the persuasive power of the musical result. 'The most striking thing was the thoroughness with which these great men made dynamic contrasts between piano and pianissimo—something which nowadays has almost disappeared. Where the dynamics were questionable—as sometimes in Strauss's own scores—he always asked us to play one or two degrees softer than he had indicated, to ensure the sound was transparent. He would never have tolerated the "inflated" sound to which I must admit his scores can sometimes seduce a conductor.'

Rudi Kempe had become aware of this early in his career. Once when Furtwängler was rehearsing Strauss's *Don Juan* with the Gewandhaus Orchestra he interrupted the love scene: 'Gentlemen, you can play that bit much softer. Here you have an oboist who plays this solo pianissimo.' More than once Furtwängler invited that oboist to Berlin, on loan so to speak. Another conductor, then regarded by Rudi Kempe as above all others for his impressive control both in technique and musicality, must have taken note of the young oboist—Otto Klemperer. More than thirty years later, during the interval of a Kempe concert at London's Royal Festival Hall, Klemperer made his way backstage and some people were anxious to introduce the two men. With an imperious gesture, Klemperer waved them aside. 'There is no need for introductions. We are old friends. This man used to play first oboe for me in the Gewandhaus Orchestra.'

That the first oboe of the Gewandhaus could also double on the cor anglais goes without saying, and on the oboe d'amore he was indispensable when it came to performing programmes of church music, which were mainly (though not entirely) devoted to the music of Bach, and given in the Gewandhaus or in the Thomaskirche. These concerts were run by the Cantor of St. Thomas's, Karl Straube, and in the years when Kempe was oboist, Straube recorded a complete cycle of Bach Cantatas for the Leipzig Radio (it is sad that none of these recordings has apparently been preserved). Although Kempe had studied Bach at source he later felt reluctant to conduct Bach's music himself, especially the choral works. 'As long as there are people like Karl Richter around, I prefer to stay at home to play Bach on my organ or harpsichord.' And so he did, for his private pleasure alone.

The concert and operatic repertoire in Leipzig naturally included many contemporary works, at least up to 1933. Of the 126 operas Rudi Kempe came to know as an orchestral player within a few years were first performances of Křenek's jazz opera *Jonny spielt auf*, Weill's *Mahagonny* and Dressel's *Rosenbusch der Maria* as well as German premières of Mussorgski's *Boris Godunov*, Stravinsky's *Petrushka* and Milhaud's *La Création du Monde*. These apart, the normal repertoire included standard works ranging from Gluck to Strauss as well as 'many things which are rightly forgotten today; but some which are sadly neglected: scores like *Tiefland* and *Königskinder*—what marvellous music! When one has to listen to what they construct today....'

In his Leipzig home, near the friendly tiled stove stood the recently delivered grand piano. But curiously enough Kempe seemed to be more at home in the theatre. When he happened not to be on duty, he stayed on simply because he wanted to know what was happening musically on stage and behind the scenes—unlike those who were in charge, the repétiteurs and members of the music staff. One day when an audition had been called they had all vanished as usual; from stage door keeper to chief conductor no one seemed to have the courage to accompany at sight on the piano the Brahms Violin Concerto—no one except Rudi Kempe. Whether it was because he hit an unusually high number of correct notes or whether it was on account of his sensitive interpretation, his so far officially unrecognised talents were about to be brought to light. A further step occurred when a Leipzig amateur orchestra called—sometimes hopefully—'Harmonie' (it drew on members of the Gewandhaus Orchestra in cases of emergency) was looking for a conductor to work with them. Nobody troubled to help them except Rudi Kempe.

So on 14th April 1934 at eight in the evening in the large hall of The Three Lilies restaurant in Cabbage-garden Street, Leipzig, he conducted his first concert. It was a totally unremarkable event. Even the programme, which gave admittance for 40 pfennigs and included the Triumphal March from *Aida*, the *Euryanthe* Overture and Smetana's *Vltava*, was by no means out of the ordinary. 'They played surprisingly well for amateurs, and for me it was fun.' It was also fun a little later on when a group of weary Gewandhaus musicians, holidaying at the seaside resort of Baabe, had sufficiently recovered to extemporise in the open air a performance of *Lohengrin* in pre-Wieland Wagner style. Rudi Kempe conducted from a hole dug in the sand.

However, life became more serious for him in the new season when one day a colleague let the cat out of the bag about Kempe's conducting to Paul Schmitz, the new Leipzig Opera Director (Gustav Brecher had been dismissed in 1935, but not for his conducting, even though that was described as a musical crossword puzzle, which he used to perform mainly behind his head; in those days in Germany people were 'dismissed' for other reasons). During a rehearsal Schmitz wanted to hear the Act II finale of *Figaro* from the back of the stalls in order to judge the balance of dynamics. Again, no assistant was there to take over. 'Kempe must do it. He's fine,' shouted one of the orchestra, in a friendly but firm way pushing his oboist colleague to the conductor's desk—and into a conducting career.

Kempe, however, still felt reluctant. He hesitated to accept the repétiteur's contract which was offered to him, not only because it would have meant a reduction in the salary he was earning as principal oboe—an important consideration for a married man—but also for another reason: 'I so much enjoyed being a member of the orchestra that I simply didn't feel like giving up my position as oboe player.'

It was characteristic of him that in decisive periods of his life he always remained passive. He simply let things happen. And they did: on this occasion in the form

Orchesterverein  Harmonie 1880

Leitung: R. Kempe

Frühjahrskonzert

am Sonnabend, den 14. April 1934, 20 Uhr, im Großen Saal der
„Drei Lilien", Kohlgartenstraße

Vortragsfolge:

Erster Teil:

1. Hymne und Triumphmarsch aus der Oper „Aida" — G. Verdi
2. Ouvertüre zur Oper „Euryanthe" . . . — K. M. v. Weber
3. Zwei Menuette
   a) Menuett . . . . — L. Boccherini
   b) Menuett aus der Symphonie Nr. 6 . . . — J. Haydn
4. Fantasie aus der Oper „Der Bajazzo" . — R. Leoncavallo

Zweiter Teil:

5. Die Moldau*), aus dem symphonischen Zyklus
   „Mein Vaterland" . . . . — R. Smetana
6. Valse romantique . . . . — M. Heineke
7. Große Fantasie „Unser Strauß" . . . . . — H. Weber
8. Marsch der Bersaglieri . . . . — R. Eilenberg

*) Aus zwei Quellen entspringt sie, plätschert munter im Gestein und glitzert in der Sonne, sie wird breiter, ihre Ufer hallen von Jagdhörnern und ländlichen Tänzen wieder. — Mondschein, Nymphenreigen. — Sie gelangt zu den St.-Johannes-Stromschnellen, an deren Felsen ihre Wellen zu schäumendem Gischt zerspritzen. Von dort strömt sie breit dahin.

Nach dem Konzert Ball!

Das Alex Heyde-Tanz-Orchester

Einlaß 19 Uhr   Eintritt 40 Pfg.

of a schedule from which he happened to discover he was to conduct a performance of *Wildschütz*—just one week after that memorable *Figaro* rehearsal. 'I had no choice. I just conducted.'

The Leipzig press found it 'hard to believe that this outstanding woodwind player is really a beginner when it comes to conducting'. Apart from his 'still somewhat over-generous beat', the critics discovered in him qualities which would have been enough for half a dozen General Directors of Music. The report concluded 'before long this remarkable talent should blossom in artistic maturity'. Rudi Kempe preferred to forget this well-meaning review. The same Leipzig newspaper some time before had been commending a Mr. Hitler for his meritorious promotion of the work of J. S. Bach so highly that a Bach medal had in fact been especially struck and presented to him.

Rudi Kempe, now seriously faced with the question of conducting, sought advice from Paul Schmitz, who must have been fully aware of what he was doing when he threw him in at the deep end and without further ado let him conduct a performance. At the Dresden Orchestral School, Rudi had learned from Kurt Striegler, then Kapellmeister at the Opera, how to play from a full score, to transpose and to acquire 'other skills that a conductor must have'; and merely by observing him he had captured something of Striegler's almost legendary stick technique. But he had never had any conducting lessons himself. Hoping to have some now with Paul Schmitz, Kempe was puzzled and disappointed to learn 'Apart from a few tips, there is nothing I can teach you' ringing in his ears. Surprisingly, he found practical help from the Gewandhaus tympanist. 'In a few moments he showed me the simple trick of relaxing the wrist and so ensuring both precision and flexibility. This was actually the only conducting lesson I ever had in my life.'

Spurred on by his orchestral friends, who good-humouredly foretold a glittering career as a conductor, he finally banished his doubts and accepted a contract as solo repétiteur and Kapellmeister. 'One can either be consistent or inconsistent, but one mustn't keep faltering all the time'—one of his 'nonsense philosophies'. To be on the safe side, he kept his oboe near at hand.

Less than ever before could Rudi Kempe complain about shortage of work now. When he was not playing in the orchestra, his hands were full of more or less inferior musical chores which ranged from operating the curtains to directing the stage bands. And when he was not at the theatre, he continued to provide chamber music for various institutions such as the Leipzig Radio or the Society of Friends for the Preservation of Hedgehogs. But above all he was kept busy dinning vocal parts into the more or less receptive heads of singers—a pastime which is called *repetieren*. This is a euphemistic description, considering that one owner of such a head needed up to seventy-six sessions, several hours long, to have a part like that of Baron Ochs in *Der Rosenkavalier* hammered into him (fortunately such extreme cases were rare). That this torture, which went on for six weeks, took place in a Bavarian weekend cottage on the Lake of Murnau, where the Ochs had invited his energetic repétiteur to spend his holiday with him, made it just bearable for Kempe.

Understandably, such a sledgehammer technique gave the young Kapellmeister welcome opportunities to study the repertoire from back to front and before long enabled him to conduct a considerable number of operas in a passable fashion. After further performances of *Wildschütz*, he had to conduct *Der Evanglimann* with Friedrich Dalberg, August Seider and Ellen Winter; *Freischütz* with Maria Lenz; *Carmen* with Camilla Kallab and Walter Zimmer; *Figaro*, this time in the complete version, and pieces like *Arabella*, *Butterfly* and *Hänsel und Gretel* which are far from easy even for a veteran. Occasionally he was allowed to conduct new productions such as Humperdinck's *Die Heirat wider Willen* (with the composer's son producing), Lortzing's *Die beiden Schützen*, Rinaldo da Capua's *Chinesische Mädchen* and other operas. And it could happen that he was required to deputise at a few hours' notice and conduct an opera he had coached but never had the opportunity to rehearse. This was the case with the often feared *Gianni Schicchi*, Puccini's only *opera buffa*. 'In those days such deputising was nothing special. We were expected to be able to do it.'

It was strange, however, that as the standard of his conducting undeniably improved, the number of performances he was given to conduct was cut down. The politics behind this experience was something which in later years he was to face more often, in one form or another. He did so with the composure that was characteristically his.

In rare moments of free time, he threw himself fully into piano playing and he tried out for himself what Bruno Walter and Furtwängler had recently begun to practise—playing piano concertos and directing them from the keyboard. Unlike Walter and Furtwängler, Rudi Kempe did not restrict himself to Bach and Mozart. Giving rein to the wilder 'Sturm und Drang' of his youth, he widened the repertoire with pieces like Weber's *Konzertstück* and Liszt's First Concerto; but for these performances he stayed in the modest setting of the 'Harmonie' Amateur Orchestral Society —to which he remained faithful for many years.

He left when he was ordered to 'dismiss' the principal viola from this orchestra, who happened to be one of the finest players.

Meanwhile it was the autumn of 1939. War had been declared.

Kempe refused to conform. His customary 'Grüss Gott' with which he would enter the theatre, his hands deliberately stuffed deep in his pockets, was not the only risk he ran and from which he somehow emerged, unable to understand how—and why—he had survived. The time he spent in military service was interrupted on occasions by desperate attempts to keep alive through music a reason for survival amid universal insanity. This time left deep furrows.

To make life spring from these furrows, to regenerate what would make life worth living, became the hope and aim of the succeeding years.

Post-War Years: an End and a Beginning

In 1945 Rudolf Kempe found himself stranded in Chemnitz. During the war he had deputised at the local theatre there as oboist and repétiteur. Later on, as First Kapellmeister, he had tried to keep the theatre going with a shoe-string staff. At that time programmes of concert and opera performances, often interrupted by air-raid alarms, had to be, by official order, more and more cheerful and buoyant—until the day when all theatres were closed.

Now Kempe stood again in Chemnitz, this time as Director of the Opera. Physically and mentally exhausted, he had a handful of singers and musicians around him, all in the same sad condition as himself. But saddest of all was the fact that their situation was no different from that of anybody else.

Accordingly, what they tried to do was no different from what anybody else did; they rolled up their sleeves and made a fresh start, in every respect. On 4th June 1945, rehearsals began, and on the 16th the first so-called 'artistic performance' took place. The evening opened with Beethoven's Egmont Overture and included prayers and tap-dancing routines. The items ranged from Gluck to Johann Strauss, including Schiller and Goethe, and were spoken, sung or danced respectively. This programme reflected everything these brave artists dared present as a glimmer of hope for their uncertain future.

The only certainty about the future was that it would not permit people to be squeamish. 'Artistic sensitivity' which could not look reality in the face with a degree of humour or a strong nerve was a luxury that could not be afforded. Reality consisted of makeshift concert halls and temporary stages without either heating or electric light, to which players and public flocked after hours of route marching through the snow and slush that covered bomb-scarred streets. Music material was in short supply, and there were no scenery, costumes or props. People listened with empty stomachs and players performed with ice-cold fingers in mittens and gloves. On many occasions their musical director conducted while wearing a woollen jacket under his evening suit and a topcoat over it. That he did not perspire at all should not necessarily be taken as a sign that his performance lacked vigour or temperament.

Kempe now capitalised on the experiences of his childhood when he had had to practise in an unheated skittle alley in his parents' inn simply because nowhere else was he undisturbed. He would never have thought of cancelling a performance because of a cold, regardless of how serious it might have been. He would rather conduct with a high temperature and afterwards run all the way from the Chemnitz Marble Palace to his home, since there was no transport—a drastic treatment which might well have had serious implications. Perhaps it was due to the experiences of this time that even in later years, when the circumstances of musical life had improved considerably, he would never cancel a performance because of any personal ailment. In fact he would have preferred to conduct with his head under his arm. Almost literally, he did so in 1946, when he was in Lugau for a performance of *Carmen*. Here the orchestra could only be squashed under the stage between supporting girders. In order to see the singers he had to stand up, and when he did so the orchestra had to follow not his baton but his legs. If he tried to bend down to the orchestra, there was no room for his head. 'Acoustically it was good training for Bayreuth....'

The Chemnitz City Orchestra provided not only Lugau with culture but also the surrounding districts, and there can be few conductors who have had the good fortune to direct *Salome* in a shooting lodge in Waldheim. Conducting in places like the churches, inns and hospitals of Schirgiswalde and Grossröhrsdorf, Kriebstein, Flöha and Seifhennersdorf is perhaps part of a necessary experience, which enables a musician to come to terms with unreasonable working conditions, such as Kempe found in later life in the Munich Philharmonic rehearsal rooms or in the Battersea and Hammersmith Town Halls. Working in such difficult acoustics, it is a miracle if one's hearing is not impaired.

In those post-war years, programmes too were not sophisticated. One had to engage whoever was available and audiences were grateful. People were so starved of culture that they readily gobbled up anything that was on the musical menu. Lieder and solo piano pieces would turn up in the middle of symphony concerts and no one would feel irritated, not even the critics. With a major work which nowadays fills a whole evening, Bruckner's Fifth Symphony for example, there were invariably coupled numerous titbits like Mendelssohn's *Midsummer Night's Dream* and Tchaikovsky's *Rococo Variations*—so that no one would leave the hall complaining of short commons. The realisation that 'Man does not live by bread alone' produced at that time results different from those of today—results which contained fewer calories and possibly more vitamins.

At least for those who lived in fear of the critics it was paradise. In those days even critics knew hunger and they too were grateful for everything that was put before them in programmes no longer interrupted by air-raid alarms but only by harmless power cuts. The phenomenon of uncritical enthusiasm even on the part of the critics was not wholly derived from the modest musical standards in Chemnitz and Seifhennersdorf (in Dresden and Leipzig at least, where Kempe was now often invited to conduct, everyone recalled music-making in better times). Anyway it was regarded as an outrage if someone reviewed a concert as a total 'write-off'. On one occasion this happened after a New Year's Eve performance of Beethoven's Choral Symphony in Chemnitz. It was reported that 'Kempe lacked the granite-like carved beats required for the classic Beethoven style', and that the Ninth Symphony was 'unsuitable' for seeing in the New Year. On reading the review the General Administrator of the Chemnitz Opera erupted and cancelled the next scheduled theatre performance and replaced it with a repeat of the Beethoven symphony. When the critic attempted that evening to enter the foyer of the packed theatre he was forcibly removed by a number of the audience. Whatever the merits of Kempe's interpretation may or may not have been, for the public it was an overwhelming success.

Fortunately, Kempe was already very self-critical in those days. He was once asked to learn Mahler's Fifth Symphony (with cuts that had been suggested to him) at a couple of weeks' notice for a concert in Leipzig where a colleague had been taken ill. 'As far as I can judge it went totally wrong. I should never have undertaken anything like that.' Henceforward he would never touch a work he did not—or not yet—feel strongly about.

His reluctance to compromise artistic standards began to attract attention, sometimes in an unpleasant way. Occasionally in different orchestras players would say of him, 'We don't want him back again, he's far too demanding for us!' And in Chemnitz the situation became intolerable when a former tenor, engaged in the same house as a producer, was newly promoted to Production Supervisor. In this position he taxed the Musical Director's patience to such a degree that Kempe decided to resign. This was shortly before the end of the 1948 season and he had no other engagement in sight. However, one should be grateful to that tenor. Four weeks later Kempe was offered an appointment at the National Theatre in Weimar.

No one could have foreseen that he was to remain there for only one season. Yet after Chemnitz, Weimar meant more to him than just a step up the ladder. After all, Weimar had a proud musical tradition founded by J. S. Bach in the eighteenth century and developed by Liszt in the nineteenth—a tradition sometimes overlooked in favour of the city's world-famous literary tradition.

As joint Musical Director with Hermann Abendroth, who worked exclusively in the concert repertoire, Kempe had a free hand when it came to opera. With a fine ensemble which included singers such as Gerhard Unger, Maria Rolle and Karl Paul, Kempe put on new productions of *Bohème, Trovatore, Tiefland* and Sutermeister's *Romeo und Julia*. To end the season and celebrate Richard Strauss's eighty-fifth birthday, he mounted a special production of the composer's last opera, *Capriccio*. For Weimar this was the first performance of a work which surprisingly at that time was played nowhere else. For Kempe this production served to strengthen his feeling for the music of Strauss, for whose *Arabella, Der Rosenkavalier* and *Salome* he already had a deep affection. However, it was *Capriccio* which he loved above the other operas. The charming 'conversation piece with music', as Strauss himself called it, seemed to go far beyond its subject matter, the supremacy of words or music. For Kempe it symbolised something decisive: the possibility of settling a centuries-old conflict in an uncontroversial and human way. This formula he tried to apply in all possible and some impossible situations....

As to the repertoire he had so far acquired, Kempe regretted that it was focused on opera and that his contract in Weimar precluded any concert work. Of course, he had enjoyed the opportunities to conduct symphony concerts given to him at Chemnitz and particularly in Leipzig (no longer with the 'Harmonie' amateurs but with the Radio Orchestra), and in his native city of Dresden the Philharmonic Society continued to invite him to conduct. However, it seemed as if the two major orchestras in Dresden and Leipzig which had reared and raised him as an orchestral musician had so far taken little notice of his breakthrough as a conductor—until one day in 1948, he received an invitation from the Dresden Staatskapelle to conduct a concert on 17th February 1949. What else could he choose to begin the programme but the *Magic Flute* Overture?

And so it happened; the love which the innkeeper's son and former O.S.K. student felt for this orchestra began to find a response in the players—an affection which lasts to this day.

Josef Keilberth, the Chief Conductor, who had initiated the invitation for that first concert, now suggested Kempe should stay on in Dresden as his personal associate with the title of Staatskapellmeister. At first Kempe hesitated whether to give up his leading post in Weimar; but when Keilberth insisted that, should he move to Dresden, he would certainly never regret it, Kempe agreed. A few weeks later, Keilberth himself left Dresden for good. His successor was Rudolf Kempe.

Dresden's celebrated opera house was a ruin, as it still is today. But on the stage of the ugly Dresden Playhouse there was assembled a group of artists who were able to revive the distinguished style of opera performances that had made Dresden world famous in pre-war years. In 1949 the company included Gottlob Frick, Christel Goltz, Kurt Böhme, Josef Hermann; Gudrun Wuestemann, Karl Paul, Elfriede Trötschel, Manfred Hübner; Arno Schellenberg, Dora Zschille, Heinrich Pflanzl and youngsters such as Gerhard Stolze and Theo Adam at the very beginning of their career. Some of these artists might well have regarded Kempe with suspicion—old troupers are often reluctant to accept a new chief in case he deprives them of their favourite long-held top notes at the very first rehearsal. But Kempe soon won their respect through his powers of persuasion irrespective of his comparative youth. Admittedly, he was nearly forty. However, 'the era when one can hold down such a job in one's twenties without having a repertoire and without having scruples about it hadn't yet begun'. Kempe was only too well aware of the responsibility which his appointment as Director of the Dresden Opera and Staatskapelle gave him, and that he chose a 'harmless' piece like *Don Pasquale* as his first new production was not necessarily derived from his liking for comic opera alone.

It did not take long for Kempe to be backed up by the orchestra itself, which still included in its ranks Johannes König as principal oboe and his old chamber-music teacher Karl Schütte as first clarinet. Many student friends from his O.S.K. days, now long-standing members of the Kapelle, followed the baton of 'their Rudi' with neither ill-feeling nor envy; on the contrary, they were proud of him. The orchestra administrator, Arthur Tröber, who controlled his players (and not only the players) with an iron hand, was nicknamed The Conductors' Grave, yet even he had to recognise the orchestra's devotion to their new chief. (Tröber was incidentally one of those who many years before had been responsible for admitting a young boy in short trousers to that fourth-floor Orchestral School.) 'They made it very easy for me, possibly because I was the first native Dresdener in living memory to become their chief.'

So the various paths of his life seemed to be meeting at a crossroads—paths which from childhood and studentship had led him back to his roots. And now at the mid-point of his life as a musician, these paths were to lead him further and further away....

Despite every obstacle Kempe was to return home again and again; and when in his concerts, even after the most exultant finale, the audience was momentarily silenced, then Rudolf Kempe and the Dresden people knew that in truth his roots were still here.

'Musically these were certainly the most beautiful years of my life—like the last moments in paradise. With opera, concerts and chamber-music evenings, I spent my entire year in one house. What a marvellous team to work with, and what an orchestra!' He often longed for those old days to return. But as Hoffmansthal writes in *Der Rosenkavalier*, 'time is a strange thing'. And Rudolf Kempe learnt the poet's philosophy 'one must not hold on to anything'.

The *Dresden Rosenkavalier* became his first gramophone recording, and it was the first complete recording ever made of the opera. It starred Margarete Bäumer as the Marschallin, Tiana Lemnitz as Octavian and Ursula Richter as Sofie. Ochs was sung by Kurt Böhme with whom Kempe—on the solid basis of debatably long-held top notes—was to strike up a lifelong friendship.

Two other complete opera productions with equally distinguished casts, made during Kempe's four years as Music Director in Dresden, are still available, thanks to the gramophone: *Der Freischütz* and *Die Meistersinger*. However, notwithstanding the obvious benefits of recording in general, the gramophone must be held largely responsible for driving music irreversibly from its original Garden of Eden which Kempe enjoyed so greatly in Dresden. In post-war Germany the calamity with all its consequences had spread more slowly than in other countries; all the more rapidly now the increasing influence of the gramophone record led music lovers in Dresden as well as in the smallest village to regard it as a poor second-best to be offered year in, year out, the same conductor, the same orchestra and the same singers in live performances, when they could have the richest choice of artists in the clinical perfection of records. From that time on the fate of musicians became that of 'fugitives and wanderers'.

For Rudolf Kempe this development had been in the offing when he was in Weimar. From here he was often invited by Walter Felsenstein, with whom he formed a valuable artistic friendship, to make guest appearances at the Komische Opera in Berlin. In 1950 his connection with the Vienna State Opera was initiated, by an agent who had been on the lookout for a singer in Dresden and happened to find a conductor instead; through him Kempe was induced to go to the Austrian capital. Soon Vienna, where he was relatively unknown, realised that 'this extremely talented young conductor could hold both stage and orchestra perfectly together without rehearsal'—even when, as once happened, his flight was delayed and he arrived at the Opera House five minutes before curtain up, to be told he was to conduct *Aida* instead of *Tosca*. Not surprisingly, Kempe came to be regarded as a tower of strength in Vienna, and for many years he conducted up to forty performances each season in the Theater an der Wien, the Redoutensaal and later in the newly re-opened Haus Am Ring.

Inevitably on his way from Dresden to Vienna, Kempe used to stop in Munich for the sake of obscure manœuvres like changing passports or seeing cabaret performances by his favourite Karl Valentin. So the previous triangular route Dresden–Vienna–Berlin began to take on a new shape, without Kempe ever planning it.

Somewhat removed from this Dresden–Vienna–Munich circuit was Barcelona. 'But I would never have had the courage to conduct my very first *Ring* at Bayreuth of all theatres; therefore I appreciated the chance of trying my hand at it in one of the lousiest opera houses in the world' (as Barcelona's is maliciously called in the trade). Singers like Max Lorenz, Gertrude Grob-Prandl, Ludwig Weber, later Bernd Aldenhoff, Kurt Böhme, Georgine von Milinkovic and August Seider were also involved in those memorable performances. 'What we experienced there was just ludicrous. However, at least I learnt *The Ring* inside out.'

In later years Kempe often asked himself why in 1952, completely out of the blue, he found himself appointed General Music Director of the Bavarian State Opera. 'I can only think that when the era of Georg Hartmann and Georg Solti came to an end, Munich was again on the lookout for a conductor who would match the General Administrator, as far as their Christian names at least.' This was the case with Rudolf Kempe and Rudolf Hartmann.

In those years Saxon dialect was more often heard in Munich than Bavarian, much to the annoyance of the locals. It was not surprising therefore that Kempe found a number of old friends at the Prinzregententheater where the opera was housed. Playing first oboe was his friend Herbert Karger (another König pupil), and from the leader's desk also came unmistakable strains of home. Another familiar face was that of producer Heinz Arnold, who in the dark days of Chemnitz had struggled for lighting and later in Dresden had mounted many successful productions together with Kempe. He also found himself rubbing shoulders with Kurt Böhme, Bernd Aldenhoff, August Seider and Gottlob Frick as well as many other 'fugitives and wanderers' who did their best to forget their nostalgia for the good old days. New contacts were made with outstanding artists like Astrid Varnay, Lisa della Casa, Hans Hotter, Herta Töpper, Marianne Schech and Hermann Uhde—contacts which were valuable in both musical and personal terms.

In addition to standard repertory performances and despite various obstacles placed in his way by the management, Rudolf Kempe mounted between 1952 and 1954 new productions of *Fidelio*, *Arabella*, Honegger's *Joan of Arc*, *Traviata*, *Liebe der Danae*,

Carmen, *Falstaff*, Carl Orff's *Bernauerin*, and *Frau ohne Schatten*. With a company including such fine artists, one might be inclined to believe that the musical standard of these productions cannot after all have been as bad as the Munich newspapers regularly tried to make out in order to put Kempe down. According to an ungenerous Munich newspaper tradition, they had done this before to Solti, Fricsay, Furtwängler and Clemens Krauss (the list is endless). But even when their campaign took the form of pamphlets couched in gutter terms (the writers used to steal terms of abuse from one another and sing them in harmony in print), they could not stifle the spontaneous acclaim which the Munich audiences unflaggingly showed their chief conductor. Kempe would only shrug his shoulders. 'What can you do with critics who prefer to hear the cymbal crash from the *Carmen* overture in the slow movement of Bruckner Seven? Personally I don't like it there!' Under no circumstances would Kempe have thought of following the advice of his well-meaning colleague, Hans Knappertsbusch, advice on the treatment of critics which cannot be repeated in print. It was not after all the press echo of the cymbal crash in his *Carmen* interpretation that 'drove Kempe from Munich', as some people tried to make out. It was the realisation of what Selim Bassa wisely says in Mozart's *Seraglio*, 'If you can't win a person's sympathy by kindness then get him out of your way', that persuaded Kempe to brush the Munich dust from his shoes—at least for the time being. With no ill feeling, and enjoying his recollections of Karl Valentin's cabaret, Kempe packed his bag and left.

When news of Kempe's long-term engagements in Vienna, Berlin, London and New York became known, the Munich press tried hard, and in a moving way, to re-appraise his abilities, which they had fiercely denied only a month before.

Thus the world was reconciled.

Two-year-old Rudi Kempe—a child like any other

First day at school, 1916

A totally unmusical family... (1922)

◁ *At the age of fourteen from the 'Tradesman's High School'—*

—to the 'Orchestral School of the Dresden Staatskapelle'. A difference of three floors only... (last but one row, sixth from left, Rudi Kempe)

Following pages:

'The usual problems with the instrument...' The young principal oboe of the Leipzig Gewandhaus Orchestra (1929)

A concert with the Gewandhaus Orchestra and the Chorus of the Lehrergesangverein under Günther Ramin in Leipzig's Thomaskirche, 1931. First oboe: Rudi Kempe

ON HOLIDAY IN THE BAVARIAN ALLGÄU
(1929–1933)

Two cups of cocoa and twelve pieces of plum cake

△ *'Ascent'—of a future conductor*

◁ *'Colleagues':
Johannes König and his pupil*

At his parents' inn 'Zur guten Quelle': the augmented 'Donnerhack Orchestra' serenading mother Kempe

'Vom Gra-a-a-al ward ich zu euch dahergesandt...' a Lohengrin performance on the shores of the Baltic at Baabe, 1934. Leader Kurt Stiehler and members of the Gewandhaus Orchestra. Conductor: Rudi Kempe

The Gewandhaus Wind Quintet:
The Kammervirtuosen   Carl Batuzat, flute; Rudi Kempe, oboe;
Wilhelm Krüger, horn; Carl Schaefer, bassoon;
Willy Schreinicke, clarinet

Piano rehearsal with tenor August Seider in the Leipzig Opera (1935) ▷

The Neue Theater in Leipzig (later destroyed in the Second World War)

Conducting his first opera performance in Leipzig, 1935

AFTER THE WAR— *With the Dresden Philharmonic Orchestra in the Christuskirche, Seifhennersdorf*

An open-air concert in the courtyard of Kriebstein Castle, a well-known T.B. sanatorium

The shell of the Dresden Opera House (Architect: Gottfried Semper)

The Dresden Playhouse (now Opera House) and the reconstructed part of Zwinger Palace

Farewell performance of Richard Strauss's 'Daphne', with Gudrun Wuestemann and Werner Liebing

△ *The Dresden music lovers are reluctant to let 'their' Rudolf Kempe go...* ▽

Preceding pages:

Chief Conductor of the Dresden Staatskapelle and Musical Director of the Dresden State Opera, 1949–1953

GENERAL MUSIC DIRECTOR OF THE
BAVARIAN STATE OPERA IN MUNICH,
1952–1954

◁ *A conversation with actress Heidemarie Hatheyer, Carl Orff and Rudolf Hartmann during rehearsals for Orff's 'Bernauerin', 1954*

▷ *After a Don Giovanni performance at the Munich Opera Festival 1954 with Lisa della Casa (above left), Erika Koeth (below, centre), Jerome Hines (behind Miss Koeth), and Benno Kusche (far right)*

▽ *New production of Arthur Honegger's 'Jeanne d'Arc' in the Prinzregententheater, 1953*

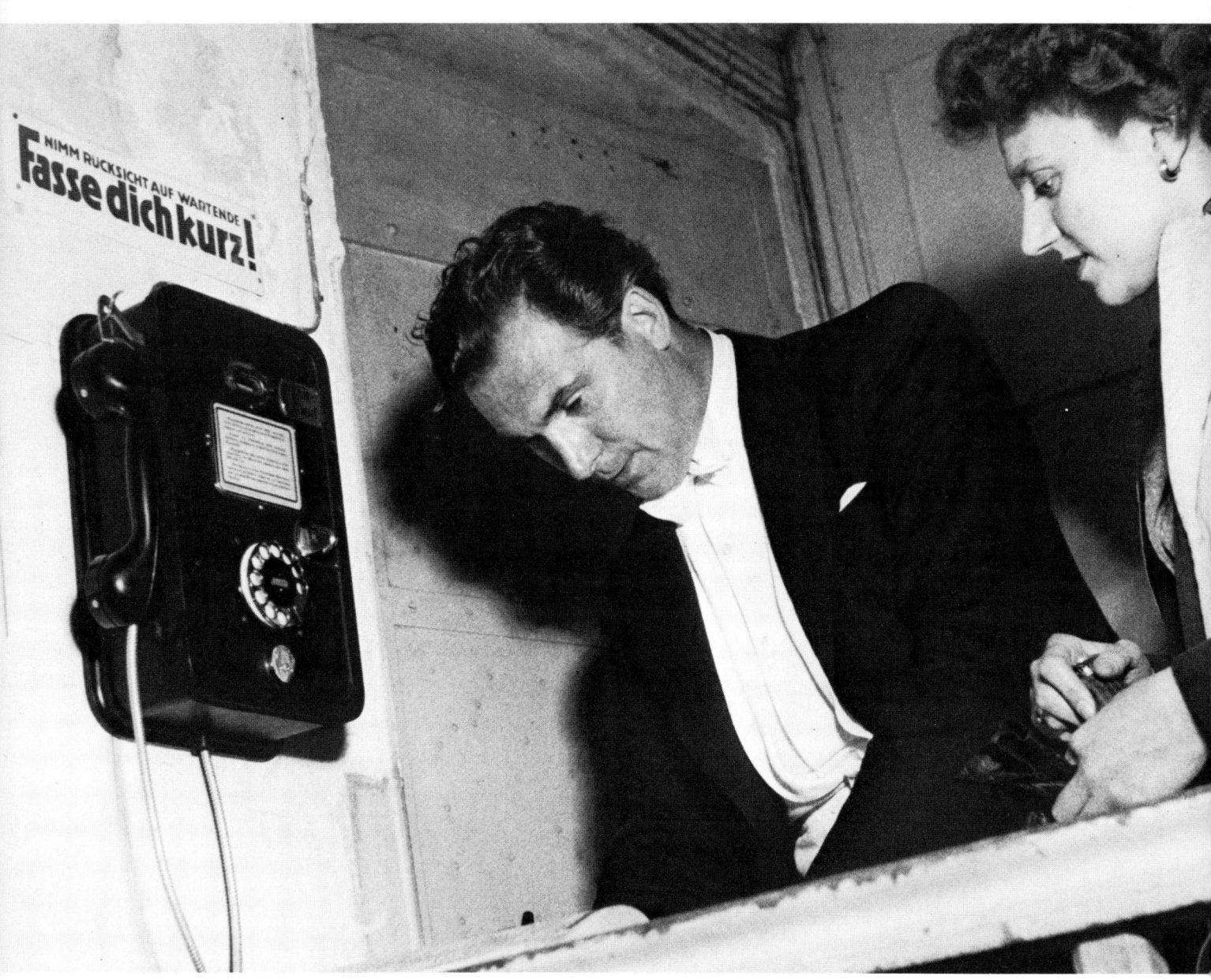

'Hanging up' on Munich ---, 1955

'Jet Set'

'All I do is fly round the world, cutting the air into little pieces....'

Of all the artists who in these years were increasingly exposed to jet-setting, Rudolf Kempe was surely the most reluctant. It was not because he disliked travelling in itself; the irritations it involved he had learned to accept with an inward groan, as he had learned long before to accept the battle with bow ties, collar studs and stiffly starched shirt fronts. All this was part of the discipline demanded by the job. His natural dislike of jet-setting stemmed rather from his realisation of a process which had started in the late forties and had become plain to him when he was Music Director of the Munich Opera. This process culminated in the break-up of ensemble theatre companies, a break-up by now irreversible. Such a harmful development was to prove particularly damaging to opera, which embraces all the performing arts, and it was keenly felt by sensitive artists like Kempe. He realised that it would be almost impossible in future to work continuously in one theatre to the standards on which he insisted.

This is why in the second half of his career the focus of his work was increasingly displaced from opera to the concert hall. In later life he was often asked whether he regretted this change of direction. 'I miss opera, of course, very much indeed, but what is the point of all this beautiful music if it can't be performed the way I want to perform it?' The idea of churning out the same old production year after year with ever-changing casts and inadequate or no rehearsal was unacceptable to Kempe. Only in theatres with a 'Stagione' system where productions are reworked intensively, no matter how few the performances, could Kempe realise his standards.

For such a Stagione he was invited by Rudolf Bing to come to the Metropolitan Opera, New York, in 1955. He was to be the first German to conduct there since the war and the Stagione included the first American performance of *Arabella*. 'That *Arabella* was new to them was evident from the first orchestral rehearsal. But already by the second I could hardly believe my ears!' And when it came to the performance the brilliance of the orchestra compared well with the standard of established 'Strauss' orchestras in Europe. In Herbert Graf's production and with Eleanor Steaber in the lead, Hilde Gueden as Zdenka and George London as Mandryka, *Arabella* became a big hit in New York. Together with his Met *Rosenkavalier* the following year, this opera was the American link in the chain on which the label 'Strauss Expert' was hung around Kempe's neck. That of 'Wagner Specialist', in America based on his Met performances of *Tannhäuser*, *Tristan* and *Meistersinger*, he somehow didn't enjoy as much in later years.

A score for which Kempe felt passionately was Hans Pfitzner's *Palestrina*. To conduct it in the Salzburg Festival production of 1955, with Max Lorenz, Ferdinand Franz, Gottlob Frick, Elisabeth Söderström, Jean Madeira and the Vienna Philharmonic, gave him special enjoyment; and six months later in New York, he heard with surprise and pleasure his colleague Dimitri Mitropoulos talking about the same Salzburg production. 'Admittedly, I was not at any of the *Palestrina* performances myself, but I am told they were lousy! I wish I knew who'd conducted them!' Kempe's smile turned into a broad grin. 'Did you hear a performance yourself?' asked Mitropoulos. 'No,' replied Kempe, 'I didn't hear them, I only conducted them.' Kempe's open laughter immediately broke the ice and rescued his colleague from his embarrassment. 'Something must have been wrong with my *Palestrina*. I'm told there were some people who actually found it quite good. Perhaps too good.' (In any case the international press reaction resounded with enthusiasm.)

In Vienna, Kempe's work with the Philharmonic Orchestra was restricted to opera (invitations to conduct concerts came only from the Vienna Symphony), and the standard of opera performances now as before suffered from lack of rehearsal. Only for new productions—Verdi's *Simone Boccanegra*, which Kempe mounted in 1951, and Werner Egk's *Revisor* in 1958—did he get the time he wanted. As for repertoire pieces, Kempe had conducted almost everything in Vienna, and surprisingly had notched up more performances of Italian operas than he was offered elsewhere. The widely held opinion that Italian music can only be conducted by Italians seemed to be one of the very few prejudices not prevalent in Vienna. Kempe's *Boccanegra*, *Otello* and *Bohème* were received with enthusiasm, and the critics wrote, 'We should try to keep Mr. Kempe in Vienna. We need someone like him at our Opera House.' Equally surprising, and for non-Viennese just as unaccountable, was another well-known phenomenon. Routine performances could on rare occasions be ravishing— 'there was just one *Fidelio* I'll never forget!'—but despite the efforts of conductor or cast they were often less than ravishing. The reasons for this did not fall within Kempe's province; and one day he left them to be tackled by the Chief Conductor designate. The latter was clearly uneasy about the Viennese enthusiasm for Kempe, who accordingly set his colleague's mind at rest by resigning. Thenceforward he came to Vienna, if at all, only to enjoy Tafelspitz and Kaiserschmarrn at the White Chimney-sweep restaurant. As far as opera was concerned, his heart was by now elsewhere.

Among the recordings he had made with the Vienna Philharmonic is one of which, contrary to habit, Kempe used to say 'This one's not bad, I don't mind listening to it. The way these Viennese play the Gold and Silver Waltz makes one want to cry for joy!' And also their joint *Lohengrin* recording, Kempe's second, worked out well, despite the difficulties Fischer-Dieskau mentions in his Preface. However, for a truly 'happy ever after' ending of that opera one has to turn to Kempe's third recording of it, a private one; it is a ten-minute version which looks back to that open-air performance on the seashore at Baabe forty years earlier. Perhaps it will be made available one day for Wagner fans with a sense of humour.

The Vienna Philharmonic's apprehension that Kempe was an operatic rather than symphonic conductor was clearly not shared by their rivals in Berlin, for an association between Kempe and the Berlin Philharmonic had steadily developed since 1955. It flourished with concerts given in Berlin as well as at the Salzburg and Edinburgh Festivals, and in many successful recordings—until one day when Kempe's persistence over 'irrelevant' details, such as the number of strings required for certain scores, met with the disapproval of the Philharmonic's Permanent Chief Conductor. However, his working relationship with the orchestra itself was always harmonious.

Rudolf Kempe could hardly have coped with the hectic activity of those years, had he not in the meantime found a new spiritual home where he felt at ease and was understood more than elsewhere.

In July 1953 he had lowered his baton for the last time as Chief Conductor of the Dresden Staatskapelle. Two months later he raised it for the first time in London—and from that moment felt at home. 'As for the language—well, that was my weak point to start with.' (At school he had only studied French.) None the less, his power of musical communication was immediately felt by the British. The rest he picked up gradually, and it was not long before passers-by in Piccadilly Circus or Hyde Park Corner would ask him of all people how to find their way around London. Since he used to walk through the London streets for hours, he had got to know the city like the back of his hand, and he would direct people correctly—with just a touch of a Saxon accent.

It had all begun at Covent Garden when the Bavarian State Opera had brought *Arabella* and *Die Liebe der Danae* to London for a guest season in September 1953. Four weeks later Kempe was invited to return alone to direct *Salome*, and six months after that, *Elektra*. *Der Rosenkavalier* followed, and when in May 1955 he conducted his first London *Ring*, Kempe's affection for the Royal Opera House was already sealed. The best singers in the world were available and he could rehearse to his heart's content, even if it was for only three performances. Furthermore it was the working spirit of the house which attracted him. From star singer to dressing-room attendant, everybody was helpful and friendly toward one another. There seemed to be only one aim—to contribute all one's ability, irrespective of personal interest, to the idea of making opera. It appeared to Kempe that the Royal Opera House—unlike others he had come to know—was free of intrigues; if there were any they must have been concealed in such a way that they could not possibly disrupt the atmosphere. Above all, Kempe discovered to his surprise that as a race the English were neither as cool nor as disinterested in the arts as the Germans commonly believe them to be. On the contrary, he found in them a lively understanding of music and a warm-hearted sensitivity that is unusual. England showed him her affection in an open-minded way which was not to be taken for granted when offered to a German. However, even a blind man could have seen Rudolf Kempe was a totally non-nationalistic and non-political individual.

It did not take long for Kempe to be invited by the other major London orchestras to conduct concerts. With the London Symphony, Philharmonia, Royal Philharmonic, London Mozart Players and B.B.C. Symphony Orchestra he regularly moved from concert hall to gramophone records, radio and television studios and back again. In between, he returned whenever he could to the charmingly old-fashioned opera house surrounded by lettuce and cauliflowers. There he conducted *Fidelio*, *Tristan*, *Butterfly*, *Aida*, and equally enjoyed *The Magic Flute*, *Un Ballo in Maschera* and his hundredth performance of *Carmen* (giving the cymbal crash with a special relish). And when in 1959 Sir David Webster asked him to direct a new production of *Parsifal*, he was deeply touched. By that time a saying had got round amongst orchestral players, and was picked up by newspapermen, 'Don't worry, Doctor Kempe is here!' This suggests that the conductor's affection for England, her musicians and audiences was reciprocated.

Therefore it was not wholly surprising when one day Sir Thomas Beecham asked Kempe to come over from Munich to discuss something with him. Kempe agreed, somewhat puzzled, and found that their discussion lasted only five minutes—just long enough for the eighty-one-year-old Sir Thomas to invite Kempe to take charge of the Royal Philharmonic. 'You have only to say yes or no, and you'll see how simple life can be.' Despite a full engagement book, the decision was simple. Twenty-four hours later Kempe said yes. That was in 1961, and so began the longest marriage he was ever to have with any orchestra.

Ten years earlier he had embarked on another orchestral marriage on the Continent with the Bamberg Symphony—a morganatic marriage only, for he was never to become their Chief Conductor, but nonetheless a happy one. The Bamberg Symphony was made up at that time of a large number of Czech musicians whose playing was still coloured by the spirit of music-making that had made Prague one of Europe's great centres of music. The warm, full sound these players produced came from warm hearts, and this made their association with Rudolf Kempe continue for a quarter of a century. During those years they undertook countless tours together, all over Europe, struggling to give of their best in all sorts of adverse conditions. Happily some of their joint performances have been preserved on record. Smetana's *Bartered Bride* is one, and Kempe rightly used to say of it, 'It would be hard to find another orchestra who could play that opera with as much spirit as these Bamberg players do!'

Somewhere on his route between dreamy Bamberg and beloved Dresden, in the picturesque countryside of Bayreuth, there lies the world-famous Green Hill. One day, in the summer of 1960, it happened that Kempe couldn't avoid stopping there. Having conducted *The Ring* not only in Barcelona but with some success in London and Munich ('I think those performances didn't go entirely wrong after all!'), he accepted Wolfgang Wagner's invitation to direct his Bayreuth production. However, the acoustics of the Festspielhaus, which are uncommonly difficult to work in, gave him—like others—little pleasure. 'After the second orchestral rehearsal I wanted to disappear for ever!' The orchestra pit, the floor of which is steeply tilted and extends far under the stage, is almost totally covered by a large cowl; this can mislead players, especially the brass section, into thinking they must play out for all they are worth. What emanates from the stage the conductor can sometimes grasp only by a process of lip reading. Yet amazingly the sound to the listener in the auditorium seems natural, when for the conductor it is totally out of balance. 'But you can get accustomed even to that, after conducting *Carmen* in Lugau!' In the event singers and players alike must have come into their own under Kempe's direction; he continued to conduct *The Ring* for the next four festivals. After an illness he returned for Wolfgang Wagner's 1967 production of *Lohengrin*; in later years he could not bring himself to sacrifice his much needed summer holiday any longer.

In the meantime Kempe had come across acoustics which in contrast to Bayreuth are enjoyable for the conductor as well as the audience: those of the Tonhalle in

Zurich. But this was not the decisive reason for his signing a contract in 1963 to become Musical Director of the Zurich Orchestra. It was above all the quality of the instrumental playing to which he soon became attached. Behind first-class woodwind players sat outstanding brass players (the number of Swiss recruits in these sections seems to be inexhaustible compared with the situation in other countries) and one could not but fall in love with the smooth sound of the strings. Possibly this was due to some native Viennese of whom the Vienna Philharmonic could have been justly proud, but possibly also to the large number of women who played in the orchestra, to Kempe's delight. 'I have the feeling that women simply make more vibrato than men!' At least for Kempe they did. An occasional un-Swiss disinclination to precision on the part of the orchestra would be discreetly counteracted by an un-Kempe-like inclination to pedantry, and was of no relevance to their joint music-making. Long after Kempe relinquished his post in Zurich the members of the Tonhalle somehow remained 'his' orchestra—until the very last day.

Another happy part of his work in Zurich was the opportunity it gave him to meet musical friends who no longer played in Germany, among them Arthur Rubinstein. Their warm-hearted musical partnership proved itself on the occasion of a concert which Rubinstein had offered to give in Zurich in 1974, at only four weeks' notice. He insisted on being accompanied by Kempe, who was not available other than for an afternoon performance, which they both normally loathed; furthermore the only chance of a run-through rehearsal was immediately before the performance. But Rubinstein, aged eighty-eight, played Mozart's D minor Concerto and Beethoven's *Emperor* with such élan and vigour that it was a splendidly enjoyable afternoon for soloist and conductor alike.

Kempe's extensive engagements were concentrated in London and Zurich; therefore he had little time for guest appearances elsewhere. Among those invitations which he occasionally accepted were concerts with Italian orchestras such as La Scala, Milan, Maggio Musicale Fiorentino and the R.A.I. Orchestras in Turin, Milan and Rome. But to be honest, it was more the beauty of the Italian countryside (irresistible to his keen photographer's eye), his liking for the Italian language (which he spoke quite well), and above all his weakness for Spaghetti al Pomodoro and Fettucine all'Alfredo which drew him to Italy. Surely Pope John, for whom Kempe had the privilege of giving a Vatican concert, forgave him his weakness for pasta, as he forgave him his Protestant outlook and attitude which unintentionally had given an ecumenical character to the proceedings.

For the most part Kempe was obliged to tour with his regular orchestras; with the Royal Philharmonic in particular he was run ragged from northern Scotland to southern Greece. He hardly ever saw more than airports, hotels and concert halls, but if he did find himself with a few hours to look around, then he would do so with an ability to absorb that was unusual. In a few moments he could steep himself in worlds completely unknown to him, such as that of classical antiquity, whether he were strolling around the Roman Forum or gazing at the ruined temples of the Acropolis. Intuitively he was able to translate all that he sensed about the ancient world into his own musical language; and his interpretations of classically inspired operas like Strauss's *Elektra* and *Daphne* were the richer for it. His intuition might well have put to shame someone who had made intensive studies of Sophocles and Euripides; Kempe had not. But if he had been aware of this gift, he would not have regarded it as anything extraordinary.

During the Odyssey of those years, Kempe was to return by recurring coincidence to places he had known and loved in his youth, such as Leipzig. The Gewandhaus as a building no longer existed, and the Congress Hall was a sad replacement for it. But the Gewandhaus Orchestra was still the Gewandhaus Orchestra, and its players were proud of their former colleague, who meanwhile had become a world-famous conductor.

His fame could not be denied even in Munich where he now returned for guest engagements, feeling neither rancour nor bitterness. Kurt Böhme's five-hundredth performance as Ochs in *Rosenkavalier* was reason enough to visit the Bavarian State Opera in their splendid rebuilt house (incidentally, Kempe had conducted many of his old friend's previous 499 performances, and there were no more debates between them about the duration of top notes). But after the sudden death of his old colleague, the conductor Josef Keilberth, Kempe found it hard to take up his baton at the same desk in the same pit to conduct the next performance. 'Rarely have I been so depressed by anything as I was by the applause which greeted me.' Yet however embarrassed he felt by it, this applause was only the spontaneous excitement about Kempe's return to the Opera House which the Munich public was expressing. And similarly genuine was the appreciation which these music lovers showed him when in 1967 he agreed to become Chief Conductor of the Munich Philharmonic.

This orchestra with a seventy-five-year-old tradition had been brought to an outstanding level of attainment by conductors such as Ferdinand Löwe, Felix Weingartner, Hans Pfitzner, Siegmund von Hausegger, Oswald Kabasta, Hans Rosbaud and Fritz Rieger. During the post-war years the orchestra had had to struggle hard for survival, and even today it still has no proper concert hall or tolerable rehearsal rooms. In spite of these setbacks, which place the Philharmonic at a considerable disadvantage compared with its rival orchestras of the Bavarian Radio and Opera, it managed to maintain its standards, thanks to Bavarian persistence and Bavarian humour. Augmented by players with similar qualities drawn from non-Bavarian parts of the world—all dubbed Prussians in Munich—the Philharmonic now achieved a real international reputation, based not only on excellent concerts at home and abroad but also on their recordings of Beethoven, Brahms and Bruckner symphonies. When the members of the orchestra with typical Bavarian self-criticism used to say 'Yes, playing fortissimo we are almost world class', Kempe would add, with good reason, 'Not only in fortissimo.'

Kempe's association with the Dresden Staatskapelle became closer again when in 1968 he embarked on a complete recording of all Richard Strauss's orchestral works. To begin with, they recorded *Ariadne auf Naxos*, one of Strauss's operas which had a special meaning for him not only musically but for its plot. What Hoffmansthal and Strauss achieved in this work—the fusion of tragedy and comedy, reconciling what seems irreconcilable—was reflected in Kempe's own personality. Only those who heard him play both Johann Strauss and Bruckner will realise this. They will understand why, when on tour an encore could not be avoided, Kempe would choose to follow Mahler's First Symphony with a piece like the Kolo from Gotovac's *Ero the Joker*. For him the D major finale of the Mahler symphony, for all its exultation, could not resolve the bitterness of the preceding movements, and he needed such a marvellously jovial piece to break the spell.

Rudolf Kempe was only too well aware of the opposing forces in himself and around him. Nevertheless he believed in the possibility of uniting them. Whether it were for the Prague Spring Festival or for the United Nations in New York, he played his part wherever he could in reconciling contradictions.

London, 1957 ▷

METROPOLITAN OPERA, NEW YORK, 1955   *Orchestral rehearsal for 'Arabella'*

Piano rehearsal with Hilde Güden (standing at the piano), Eleanor Steber and Brian Sullivan; at the piano Tibor Kozma

After the First Night and American première of 'Arabella' with Hilde Güden, Eleanor Steber, George London, John Gutman, Blanche Thebom and producer Herbert Graf

SALZBURG FESTIVAL 1955
'PALESTRINA' BY HANS
PFITZNER

*Orchestral rehearsal with
Vienna Philharmonic*

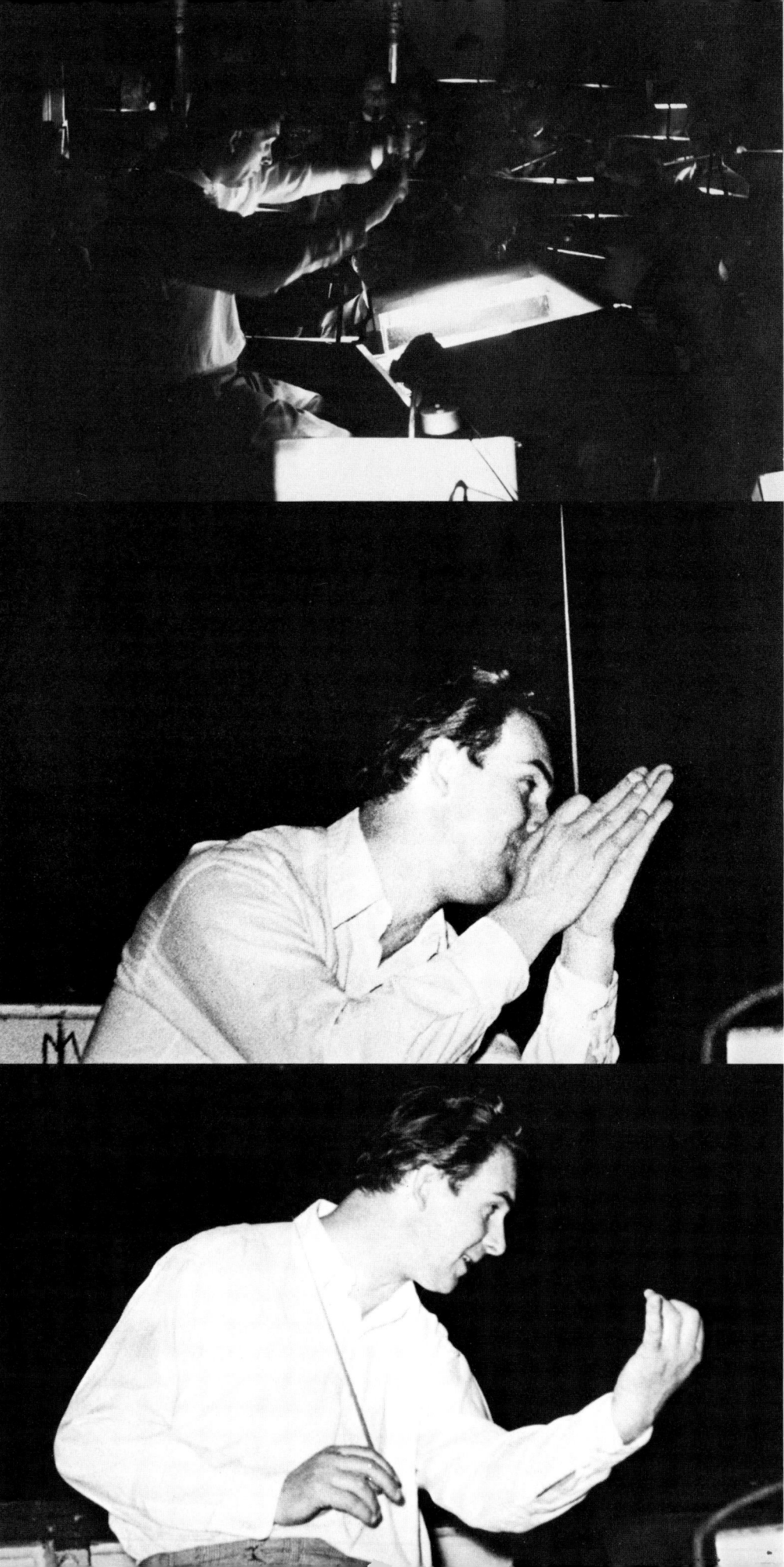

Jean Madeira (Silla)

Elisabeth Söderström (Ighino)

Talking to the composer's widow and to Max Lorenz (Palestrina)

Recording sessions with Vienna Philharmonic in the Musikvereinssaal (1958)

Rehearsing the new production and Austrian première of Werner Egk's 'Revisor' for the Vienna State Opera in the Redoutensaal, 1958

*Recording Brahms's Violin Concerto with Yehudi
Menuhin and the Berlin Philharmonic, 1967* △▽ *Royal Opera House, Covent Garden, London* ▷

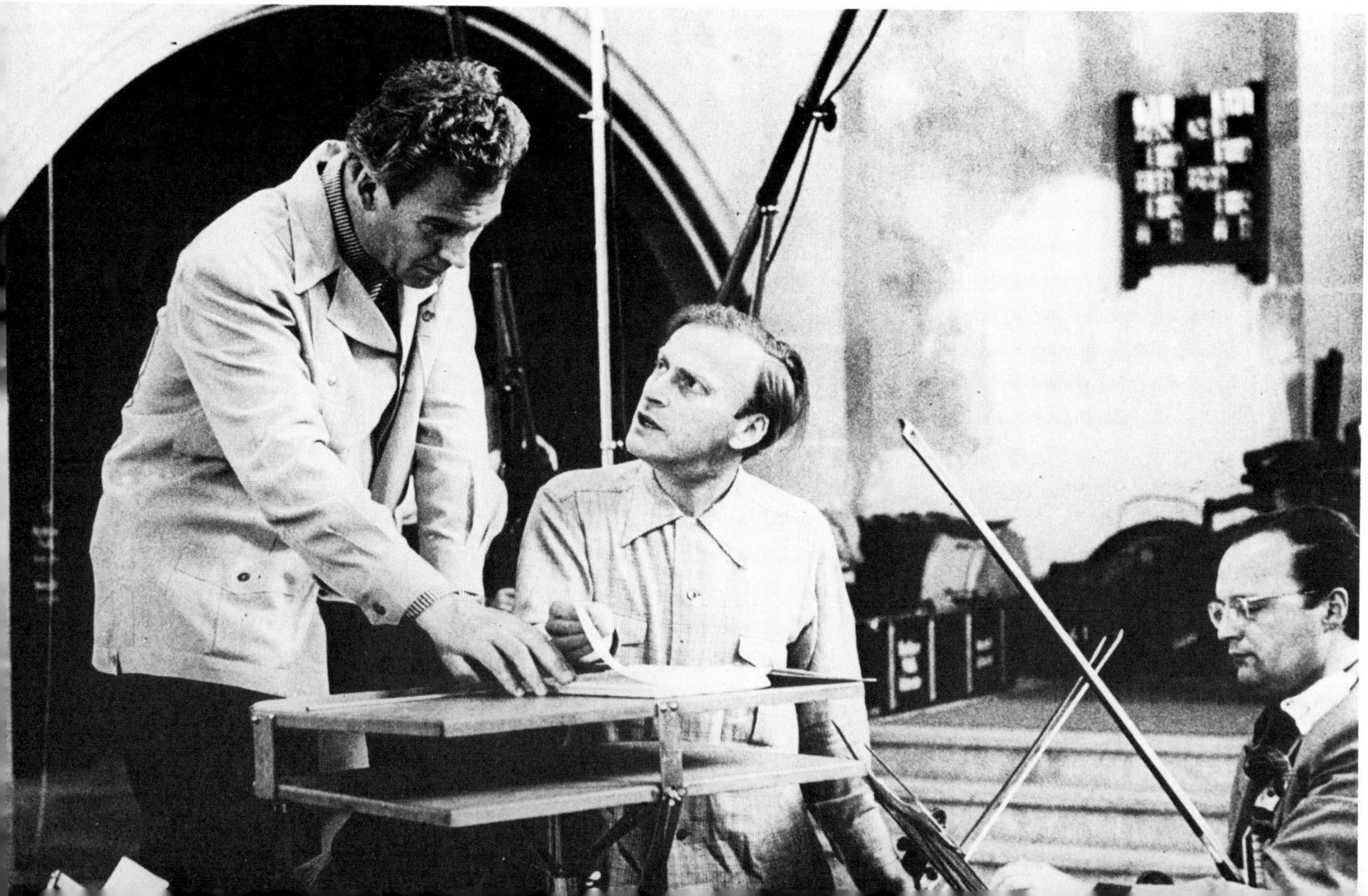

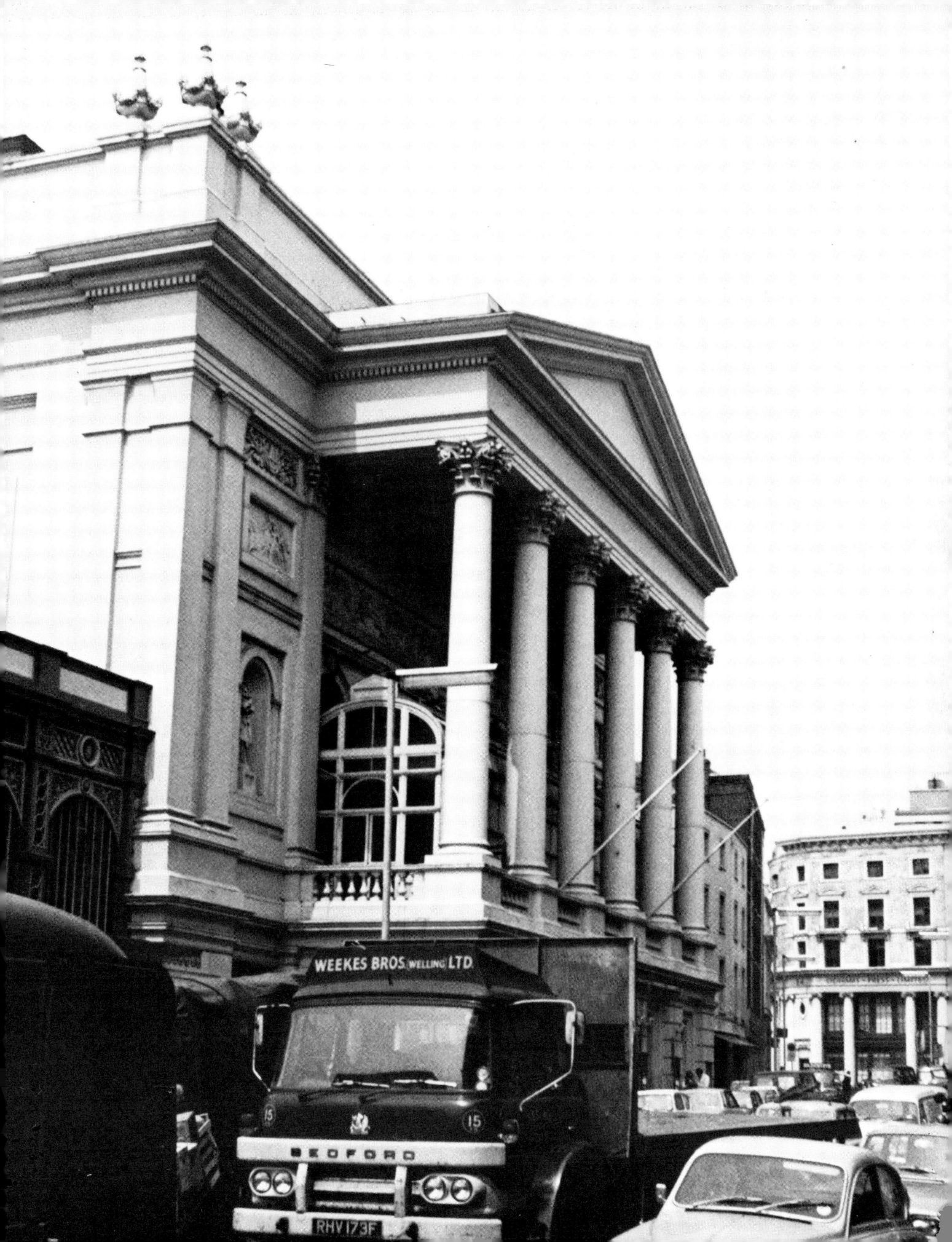

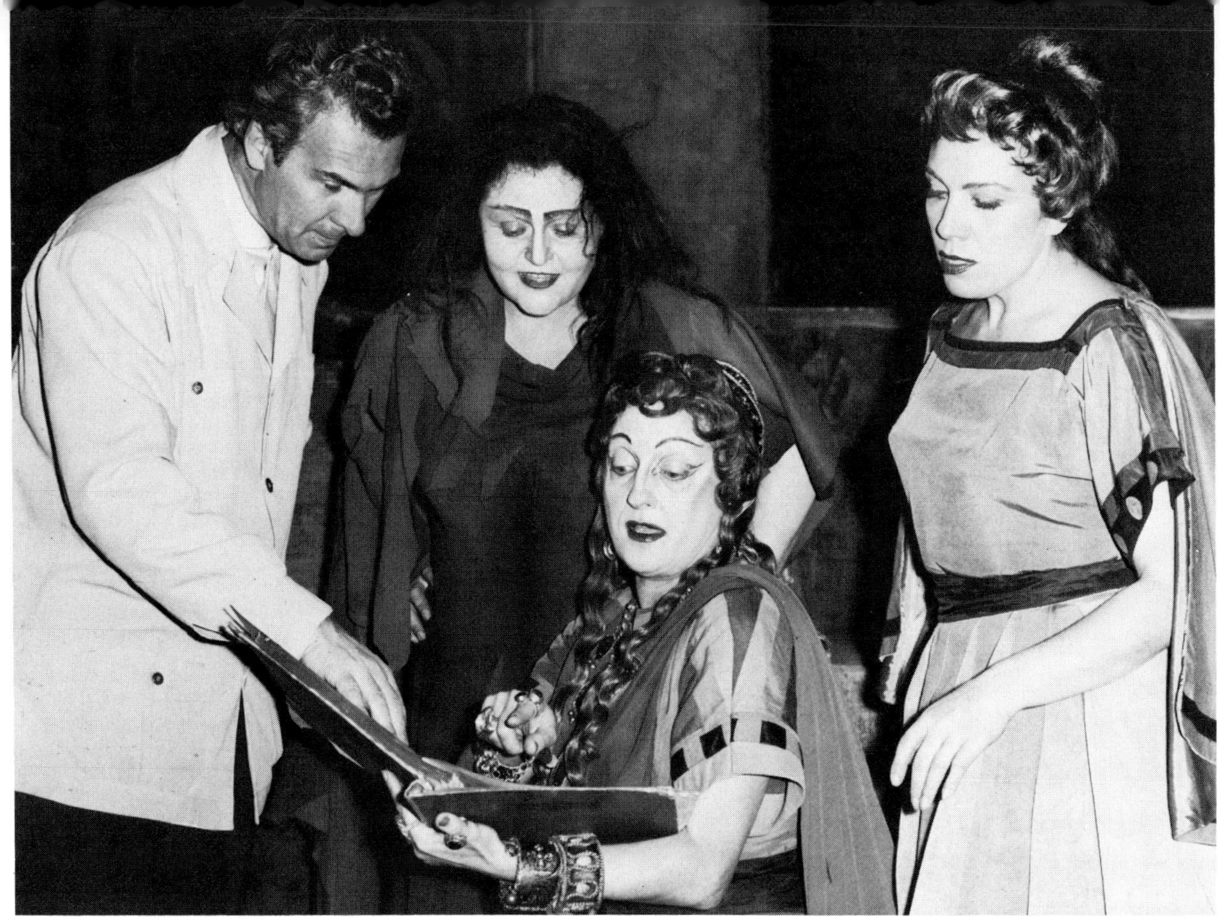

*New production of 'Elektra' with Gerda Lammers (Elektra), Georgine von Milinkovic (Klytämnestra)
and Hedwig Müller-Bütow (Chrysothemis)*

'PARSIFAL', 1960

Backstage with Gerda Lammers (Kundry) and producer Herbert Graf

Dress rehearsal

With the orchestra

'LOHENGRIN' RECORDING, VIENNA, 1963

With Dietrich Fischer-Dieskau and Christa Ludwig at a playback

Soloists Elisabeth Grümmer, Jess Thomas, Gottlob Frick, Dietrich Fischer-Dieskau and Christa Ludwig, the Vienna State Opera Chorus and the Vienna Philharmonic

Royal Festival Hall, London

First rehearsal with the Royal Philharmonic Orchestra as successor to Sir Thomas Beecham, 1961

An R.P.O. concert in the Royal Festival Hall, London (the National Anthem)

The very first ladies ever to be appointed to the R.P.O.
('Thank goodness—orchestras without women always remind me of the army!')

The conductor in the organ mirror of the Festival Hall

A concert in Bad Kissingen, 1960

THE BAMBERG SYMPHONY ORCHESTRA

Recording session for Smetana's 'Bartered Bride', 1962

Playback, with Fritz Wunderlich

Following pages: BAYREUTH 1962. *Orchestral rehearsals ('almost everything is too loud!')* ▷

'Rheingold' piano rehearsal with Kenneth Neate (Loge), 1963

BAYREUTH 'RING', 1960–1963

On stage with producer Wolfgang Wagner (far right), 1961

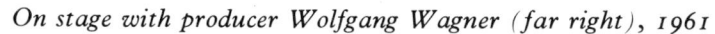

Zurich, 1963

Flowers for the newly appointed Musical Director of the Tonhalle Orchestra

◁ *A concert in the Tonhalle, Zurich* ▷

Rehearsing with Arthur Rubinstein ▽

A concert with the R.A.I. Orchestra, Rome, in the Vatican—

◁ *St. Peter's* ROME, 1963

—for Pope John XXIII

Athens, the Acropolis

With the Royal Philharmonic Orchestra in the Theatre of Herodes Atticus, Athens Festival 1965

Rehearsing with Annerose Schmidt and the Gewandhaus Orchestra in Leipzig, 1965

During the break, with daughter Maria
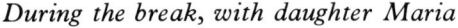

Applause in Leipzig

Back to Munich—Kurt Böhme celebrating his 500th performance as Baron Ochs in Strauss's 'Rosenkavalier'
Left to right: Erika Köth (Sophie), Herbert List (Artistic Manager), Herta Töpper (Octavian), Kurt Böhme (Baron Ochs) and Ingrid Bjoner (Marshallin)

Chief Conductor of the Munich Philharmonic, 1967 ▷

RECORDING STRAUSS'S
'ARIADNE AUF NAXOS'
IN DRESDEN, 1968

◁ *Gundula Janowitz (Ariadne)*
▽ *Sylvia Geszty (Zerbinetta)*

◁ *The Dresden Staatskapelle in the Lukaskirche*

▽ *Playback. Front row: Sylvia Geszty; behind her Teresa Zylis-Gava, on Kempe's left Theo Adam, Gundula Janowitz, Recording Producer Dieter-Gerhard Worm (with score), and Peter Schreier*

Rehearsing with the R.P.O. (soloist: Derek Wickens, oboe) in the Smetana Saal

PRAGUE SPRING FESTIVAL 1969

Autographing at the conductor's desk

Piano concerto with Rudolf Serkin

THE R.P.O.'S NORTH AMERICAN TOUR, 1969
THE 25TH ANNIVERSARY CONCERT FOR THE UNITED NATIONS IN NEW YORK

Interval conversation: Benjamin Britten, U Thant and Rudolf Serkin

Gustav Mahler's First Symphony in the United Nations' Auditorium

Man and Musician

During those restless post-war years, many artists fell victim to jet-setting—a maelstrom which washed up a lot of mediocrities and drowned some talents.

What saved Rudolf Kempe from becoming one of these victims was not least his peace of mind. This inborn gift he had developed by conscious effort during the first half of his career—a career which was by no means spectacular. In its course he had come to realise that 'conducting cannot be learnt. It can only be experienced.' The sum of these experiences allowed him to focus his energy on music, and to concentrate his attention entirely on the orchestra, free from any technical or theoretical problems whenever he was conducting. It also spared him the necessity of spinning on the 'roundabout of vanity' which too often nowadays is what the conductor's rostrum has become. At a time when people, misled by commercialism, try to idolise artists in a way that has little to do with appreciation of music, Kempe was one of the very few to uphold the integrity of music and of his personality. Even more, he was able to give strength to others and point to standards which alone could meet the demands of the present, because they were rooted in the past. Most of those who came in contact with him sensed this, and for him there was no need to prove it otherwise than through the way he made music.

As a result, many orchestras tried to put Kempe in charge, and there were three of the major orchestras in Europe which actually succeeded in winning his services. He was in demand for his personality as an interpreter as much as for his recognised abilities as an orchestral trainer. Kempe appreciated having regular engagements with the same orchestra. It allowed him to concentrate on a few places only, where he could build a steady working relationship with the players. In any case, he disliked what increasingly became a fashion not only among conductors: to travel here and there picking the largest plums out of the pudding. Kempe's attitude may have surprised people, when he turned down 'star' engagements in order to fulfil routine concerts with his regular orchestras. Remarks like one made when he was laid low with 'flu, 'What do you expect if he's greedy enough to have three orchestras at the same time?' were incorrect, and not just from the medical point of view. Kempe believed it made more sense for all concerned if he conducted twenty concerts a year with each of his three orchestras instead of conducting three concerts with twenty different orchestras. It was better too for his health, which after two serious illnesses needed care and consideration. The war and post-war years had taken their toll of him physically and mentally. If later he regained full health, it was only by keeping at bay all that could weary him. With an iron will and self-discipline he preserved his strength.

What the press used to call 'Kempe's Empire' consisted of the Royal Philharmonic, the Zurich Tonhalle Orchestra and the Munich Philharmonic. Because the characters of these orchestras, due to different traditions and working conditions, vary greatly, each makes different demands on a conductor. The structure of the two continental orchestras has been proved over many years and financially both are sound. They are supported by an audience of regulars whose attendance is based on a subscription system, a fact that has great influence on the character of an orchestra and its style of playing; security may ensure an organic development and a continuous sense of working together, but it also carries the danger of staleness. In Great Britain the situation is different. In London alone there are five first-class orchestras which receive little financial support from the Government and are almost totally dependent on living from hand to mouth in competition with one another. Musicians are engaged without full-time contracts and there are no pension or benefit schemes. Instrumentalists move from orchestra to orchestra and are under constant pressure to give their best in all kinds of adverse circumstances. Furthermore, there is no guarantee of support on the part of the audience because there is no subscription system. Almost every concert has the sword of Damocles hanging over it, since everything depends on box-office receipts.

Whether on the Continent or in England, it is the responsibility of the Musical Director to keep in balance the positive and negative consequences of these different systems. Programme building is only one of the factors in the equation, which can be almost impossible to solve unless the conductor can bring to the problems a considerable breadth of experience, prompt reaction to changing circumstances, unselfishness and personal artistic skill of the highest order.

Clearly the conductor's repertoire plays an important part, and Rudolf Kempe's was remarkable. He had studied more than a hundred operas from various perspectives and had thus developed not only his technical skill and assurance but also flexibility and versatility in style. His concert repertoire consisted of some seven hundred works of all periods, and it is evident that such a number must have included many by contemporaries—which never led to any problems, thanks to his technique. If, as was sometimes said, he conducted too few contemporary works, one of the reasons was that he felt the field should be left to people who feel more at ease in modern music than elsewhere. Furthermore his long years of experience had convinced Kempe that more could be achieved by evolution than revolution—at least in the concert hall. If an audience that disapproved of everything composed after Brahms suddenly and enthusiastically accepted a 'difficult' work like Mahler's Ninth Symphony, then Kempe was sincerely pleased. His strategy of juxtaposing small doses of modern music alongside established classics often converted audiences to works going further than Mahler's Ninth, as happened in conservative Munich and over-conservative Zurich. In London, however, the doses had to be measured even more carefully. Only the B.B.C. Symphony Orchestra, of which Kempe became Chief Conductor in 1975, is financially more independent than the others and thus has the opportunity and—to some extent—the obligation to promote modern music. As a result, however, this orchestra was perhaps over-exposed to contemporary scores during the early 1970s, and now looked to its new Chief Conductor to redress the balance and reinstate a mainly classical and romantic repertoire. Kempe didn't object to this. After all, his liking of modern music usually ended 'where no more sounds are left, only noises'—a sentiment he never tried to hide. 'What can be controlled only with the aid of a stop-watch should be conducted by a traffic warden and not by a musician. In my opinion, this belongs to the fairy-tale world of the Emperor's Clothes.'

Nevertheless the variety of Kempe's programmes hardly left anything to be desired, despite the limitations on rehearsals and casting, and other common irritations caused by financial restrictions. Attempts to take on tour interesting programmes requiring extra wind and percussion players as well as additional rehearsals mostly ran aground not only through lack of resources but because of the pig-headedness of the local entertainment officers. With their perpetual requests for Beethoven's Seventh and Brahms's First, they almost wrecked Kempe's nerves, despite his great love of these two symphonies. Wherever he could he persistently tried to bring more variety to 'grey mausoleum' programmes. And if he largely succeeded, it was not least because he personally had no special likes or dislikes in music. 'Actually, I always most enjoy the music I am making at the moment. Pieces I have no feeling for I simply try to avoid!' One-sidedness bored him, and he sometimes groaned when as a 'Strauss expert' he was asked again and again to perform works like *Heldenleben*, *Zarathustra* and the *Alpine Symphony*—the last a score especially beloved by non-alpine people. Fortunately, Kempe's love of Strauss's music was undying. The mammoth pieces of this composer were never in danger of sounding trivial under Kempe's direction, thanks to the subtlety he achieved in grading tempi and the transparency in balancing dynamics. What he particularly liked about them was their soft endings. The notion that 'the louder a concert ends, the greater will be its success'—often rejected by Strauss but commonly practised nowadays—was something that very much went against the grain with Kempe. In that context he fought many battles for the scores of Haydn, Mozart and Schubert, composers to whom he perhaps felt closer than to those with whom he was commonly associated. Above all he disliked the fashion of placing their symphonies before the interval, more or less as warming-up pieces, so that they seemed totally out-weighed by heavier second-half scores—a fate which to Kempe's annoyance sometimes even befell Brahms's Third Symphony.

For the so-called classics in modern music, Bartók, Hindemith and Stravinsky, Kempe had a special affinity, but he also greatly enjoyed conducting Prokofiev, Kodály and Janáček. Among these eastern composers Shostakovich was perhaps the closest to him—as close as Bruckner and Mahler. The latter two composers, whose symphonies were rarely performed in England before the Second World War, now enjoy a particular interest here—a development for which Kempe, although he would never claim it, could rightly take some of the credit. In return, his habit of playing forgotten or somewhat disregarded works by composers like Respighi or Korngold, Mohaupt or Revueltas, was a foible his audiences forgave him.

Nearly two hundred works from his concert repertoire, some of them lasting over an hour, Kempe would conduct from memory. For the rest, he preferred to 'read' them in Knappertsbusch style. When asked why he would not conduct from memory, Knappertsbusch had once replied ironically, 'You see, I can actually read music.' So could Kempe, and what is more, his scores were readable. Compared with some scores he came across in orchestras or opera houses, which are so peppered with coloured markings as to be illegible, Kempe's own scores seem almost untouched. His thin and sparse pencil markings of tempi and dynamics never obscure the music—not even visually.

Although Kempe preferred to conduct from memory whenever possible, he would never do so if any risk was involved, for instance that of a soloist's confidence. This confidence can be jeopardised by a conductor conceited enough to accompany without having the score on the stand. 'This is something one mustn't do under any circumstances. Admittedly, conducting from memory certainly permits a far freer style of music-making, and above all contact with players is more intense when a conductor does not bury his head in the printed page. Whenever he uses a score, a conductor should know a piece well enough to look at the music only in case of emergency, so to speak. For me, contact through the eyes with each of the players is of the greatest importance. In this way, one can give a player a greater degree of security'—on condition of course that the conductor himself is absolutely secure. Kempe would never have dared to go on to the concert platform if he had not in fact known every note of the score. To conduct a piece of which one has only the vaguest knowledge and to be surprised by what does or does not come out of the orchestra is a venture for which Kempe was too conscientious. 'God help us if only one woodwind player, no matter how minor his part may be, makes a mistake! Players can have a blind spot at any moment, I must not.' Kempe's musicians, who often asked themselves why he never made a mistake in his beat, may have regarded this as the only inhuman quality they could discover in him. However, it was less the result of his staggering memory than of his conscientiousness in re-working again and again what on his level is normally regarded as mere routine.

Perhaps this was one of the reasons why in all circumstances he won such confidence in guiding an orchestra, at a time when everywhere, not only in orchestral life, people—often rightly—are kicking against the pricks of authority. The musicians knew that Kempe would demand more from himself than from all the others put together. 'I believe each orchestra has the right to have good conductors. Every player has to prove he has learnt his trade and be heard in every bar. Only the conductor cannot be heard. And many a conductor stands on the rostrum, by no means sure of his ground, making a big fuss at the expense of the orchestra, who may have had to save him from disgrace. If, in such cases, players rebel, they have my sympathy. They should have the chance of choosing whom they want to confide in, and not be presented with someone by politicians as often happens! Democracy in orchestras is absolutely vital—and it works if it is based on mutual respect which everyone has to pay to the efforts of others.' However, the responsibilities and duties Kempe assumed as conductor and director of an orchestra required him to retain certain rights in artistic decisions such as the engagement of players, the selection of programmes and soloists and the scheduling of rehearsals. On the few occasions when he found himself forced to resign from a theatre or orchestra it was on account of incompetent administrators whose interference made it impossible for him to exercise his responsibility any longer. 'These matters actually never had anything to do with my contact with the players or with our partnership. So we could continue to make music together, even after a separation.' This was a realisation which made him happy.

His Royal Philharmonic endeared themselves to him for their brilliance, for being typically English in the speed and accuracy with which they understood and followed him, and above all for their virtuosity. 'They are like full-blooded racehorses: you can't hold them back. They have temperament. There is no need to drive them either—they are always ahead.' This was amazing when one considers their schedule—a schedule which would make any player in a continental orchestra gasp. That they unflaggingly undertook two and sometimes three three-hour sessions a day, often in different locations which could be miles apart, is something that could stem only from their good humour. The fact that the conductor also had to exist with only a sandwich in his stomach from morning to night served to make the personal bonds between Kempe and his musicians even closer, as did—after a six-hour bus journey with them from Philadelphia to New York—the condition of his trousers as crumpled, his joints as stiff as theirs. (How he relaxed in time for the evening concert was his secret.) And when in performances after such a journey, the chorale-like trombone solo in the finale of Tchaikovsky's *Pathétique* rang out as if from another world, or the lady flautist embroidered her variation in the passacaglia of Brahms's Fourth Symphony with indescribable beauty, or the violas expressed the sadness in the slow movement of Bruckner's *Romantic Symphony* with compelling intensity—then players and conductor realised how much they complemented one another.

After a fifteen-year association in which he had been loyal to them throughout, the Royal Philharmonic's 'conductor for life' would never have left the orchestra of his own volition. When events over which he had no control forced him to resign, he was deeply depressed.

It was several months later that Kempe accepted an offer to become Chief Conductor of the B.B.C. Symphony, an orchestra very familiar to him through many guest appearances with them over two decades. The affection which the B.B.C. players now gave him went deeper in his heart than was shown on the surface. Among the few concerts that they were able to give together were several in which 'it' happened—something that cannot be explained. Even the most unmusical person in the world cannot escape from it, and somehow it makes everyone happy, if only for a few moments. Schubert's Fifth Symphony, his A♭ Mass, Janáček's Sinfonietta and even the New World Symphony, played no matter how many hundreds of times before, created such moments—not least through the Prom audience, an English phenomenon which, thanks to the pioneering of Sir Henry Wood some eighty years ago, and nowadays supported by the B.B.C., gives to the Prom concert series an atmosphere quite unique in the world. 'If during the whole summer thousands of young people

—after queuing for cheap tickets for up to twenty-four hours—flock every night to the ugliest concert hall ever built, if the moment the conductor appears their boisterous frolics suddenly turn into breathtaking silence—a silence lasting through demanding programmes of sometimes three hours' length—if this silence at the end bursts out into a frenetic applause which elsewhere in the world is heard only at football games—well, then I know why we are making music.' The typically English characteristic of these spectacles is the total lack of hysteria which in other countries would inevitably be felt; and even the T-shirt slogan 'Kempe for King' displayed by some of the promenaders was nothing but a joke, and left no doubt that the owners of those T-shirts in the first place enjoyed music itself.

If Kempe felt at home in England it had little to do with the rather obscure historic connection between Angles and Saxons—though a Saxon himself he didn't trouble about that. Perhaps it was not even due to the fact that London is today undeniably the centre of the music world. Possibly it was because some of the fundamental characteristics of Kempe's nature seem to have been invented in this country—characteristics like discipline and tolerance, tact and sense of humour.

What he sometimes subconsciously missed in the style of English orchestras was a certain weight required by the music of Brahms and especially Bruckner; perhaps it must be inborn. This he found in his Munich orchestra, together with a way of music-making which in its flexibility was based not so much on elegance as on a special depth of feeling—with some reservations one could call it German. Whatever it is, this quality made it a pleasure for Kempe to perform with this orchestra, apart from Beethoven and Brahms, works of the late Romantics. Pieces for small orchestra—Stravinsky's *Pulcinella*, Strauss's *Bourgeois Gentilhomme* and his *Metamorphoses*—became delicacies, thanks to the distinguished principals. Surprisingly these 'Bavarians' were equally at home when it came to waltzes and light music: the slight rhythmic distortion of the basic one, two, three pattern which gives the waltz its lovably loose character—'something one shouldn't analyse or it becomes exaggerated'—is a speciality of the Munich Philharmonic. With it they obviously disprove the theory that Munich owes its reputation as a suburb of Vienna solely to its fondness for intrigue. The opposite, somewhat egotistic, theory that Vienna is just a suburb of Munich may contain a grain of truth due to the authentic manner in which Bruckner's symphonies are on occasion performed in Munich. Under Kempe, the Philharmonic achieved a number of performances of that calibre, not only in Munich but in London, Leningrad and Geneva. Their recordings of Bruckner's Fourth and Fifth Symphonies genuinely capture this quality—rather surprisingly when one learns that the sessions took place in a brewery. Recording proceeded against the creaking of the central heating apparatus which never functioned properly and against the thunder of crashing plates dropped in the adjacent kitchen during pianissimo passages, ruining otherwise successful takes. Furthermore, it was impossible to close the door between the smelly beer hall and the shoe-box recording room which had not been aired since it was built. During the breaks, when the players tried to tune up or practise difficult passages, the conductor could not listen to takes, and the playback likewise made it impossible for the players to hear themselves. However, the sacrifice of nerves and good humour exacted by these conditions was gladly made by conductor and orchestra alike, and the quality of the results they achieved, for all that, induced the City of Munich to spend the money earmarked for a concert hall on the roof of the Olympic stadium instead.

As far as the surroundings were concerned, recording sessions in Dresden were more enjoyable for Kempe (if recording could ever be enjoyable for him at all...). The studio in the Lukaskirche has a control room which, unlike Munich, technically leaves nothing to be desired. Furthermore, it can be aired at any time, and offers a friendly, almost open-minded atmosphere with international posters and street signs on the walls, emphasising English connections. The church where the orchestra plays possesses an excellent heating system, and instead of nerve-racking kitchen noises, it contributes melodious peals from its bells. Slightly re-coloured, these chimes might well have been used in the *Alpine Symphony* for cow-bell effects. These and other technical tricks would have created no problem for the Dresden recording team, which Kempe regarded as the best he had ever worked with; unfortunately their ability in this direction remained unexploited, particularly when working with Kempe and the Staatskapelle. (The orchestra still called him Chief, a habit which these conservative players could not break after more than twenty years.) If for reasons of casting or non-availability a recording had to be broken off and could only be continued a year later, then the new takes, unrehearsed, still blended perfectly with the previous ones in balance, mood and expression. And if a passage had to be repeated due to an unscheduled outburst of bell ringing, then the brass section would play after six hours of recording as freshly as at the beginning of the session. (They had to follow this of course with their regular opera performance in the evening.)

During these years, in which Kempe recorded the complete orchestral works of Richard Strauss 'down to the last dregs', the Dresden orchestra proved itself to be far more than 'the' leading Strauss orchestra in the world—a title they owe to the springy elegance of their playing, the warmth of their string sound, the unusual balance of their wind sections and, above all, the transparency they bring to any score, no matter how thickly textured it may be. When, for a welcome change from recording, the orchestra gave concerts with Kempe in Dresden's Cultural Palace, it was hard to decide which of their interpretations one would prefer—Beethoven, Tchaikovsky, Debussy or Stravinsky. Even Mahler, whose music, surprisingly, they are not fond of, they used to play with such delicacy and sensitivity that Kempe threatened, 'Just you wait! I'll get you all used to him yet!' And on New Year's Eve when this 'band' let off the most brilliant volleys of operetta fireworks, they turned the whole of Dresden into a sparkling topsy-turvy version of *Flederkavalier* and *Rosenmaus*, and one could be forgiven for thinking this the culmination of all music-making.

To the Zurich Tonhalle Orchestra 'where the slow movement cor anglais solo in the New World is played more beautifully than anywhere else', Kempe returned as often as he could during the last years. Having rid himself of the Chief Conductor's burdens (bureaucracy in any form had always been a nightmare to him) and in consequence permitting the 'no smoking' sign in the committee room to be taken down, he could now make music with the Tonhalle Orchestra for their unspoiled mutual pleasure.

He hardly ever undertook guest appearances with other orchestras, not just for lack of time. More than ever Kempe hated the life of a nomad, and more than anything he loved to be in his homes in Munich and Zurich where he could lead his own very simple life. He adored home-cooked meals, enjoyed the freedom to mess around in casual clothes and above all to fiddle with the dishwasher—a pastime which was his undisputed prerogative. The consequences sometimes slightly upset the smooth running of the kitchen, but always found forgiveness. In London Kempe lived in a hotel, but he consoled himself with the fact that his socks could be put in the same drawer, year in, year out, and that *The Times* would be meticulously laid on his plate at breakfast always by the same friendly waiters (his dislike for printer's ink led him to remove it immediately). Above all he appreciated the inimitable and very English blend of cordiality and reserve with which the customs officers would ask him on his arrival at Heathrow whether this time he were going to perform Mahler or Shostakovich—two composers whose music is not always distinguished, even by experts, without the benefit of a programme.

What seriously bothered Kempe was 'the nuisance that nowadays every orchestra regards it necessary to tour as often as possible. Under considerable strain, they give concerts after which they're reported to have played better than the local orchestra (which they believe anyway) or worse (which they don't want to know).' Since this 'nuisance' seemed imperative for the prestige of an orchestra, Kempe reluctantly accepted it, seeking amends in the harvest of photographs or cine films he hoped to take home. When, as happened on his last North American tour with the R.P.O., he had the chance of taking his grown-up daughters with him (as a special concession they had been let off their professional and family duties) he had a wonderful time strolling, sight-seeing and, if he were free in the evening, going to plays and musicals. His pride in 'his girls' even outweighed the slight touch of embarrassment he felt as he steered his harem through the Manhattan crowds. Fortunately any lift-boy could have spotted that at least two of his escorts were relatives.

Just as necessary for the prestige of an orchestra as touring, so people tried to convince him, were certain set exercises in publicity. For Kempe these duties were a drudgery. If he were dragged to a party or reception, the local dignitaries would hardly have a chance to welcome him before he would vanish through the nearest door. If a reporter, assisted by conspiring members of the orchestra, managed to smuggle himself into the conductor's room, his questions on how Kempe might like this particular festival inevitably received the icy retort 'I loathe festivals'.

'After all, most interviews only seem to offer journalists a chance to hang someone else's name on their own ideas.' This matched Kempe's experience and opinion of concert reviewers. 'If critics would only admit that they are human beings too and that their views are personal, then it would be possible to accept their criticism, be it favourable or unfavourable, as constructive. But when the opinion of one person is declared compulsory for everyone, I begin to question it. Criticism can hardly be objective: everybody feels and reacts differently since their moods and dispositions vary, whether they are performing or listening. Far more important than any other criticism, I think, is self criticism.'

Kempe hardly ever gave interviews. In the few he did give, he was invariably asked the same question: 'As a conductor who has worked with almost every top-ranking orchestra in the world, what do you think are their different characteristics?' In answering he would try to do justice to each by referring to their various qualities. When asked if there were any one orchestra which boasted all these qualities, he would respond only with a smile. But when in a performance of *Heldenleben*, his eyes met those of the Dresdener's principal double bass player, who was listening with ill-concealed emotion to the beautiful violin melody in the coda, and again when after a playback the recording manager would ask 'Is it all right, Mr. Kempe?' and Kempe in a slightly unsteady voice would answer 'For me, it is'—then the same smile would shine on his face.

The project of recording all Strauss's operas with the Dresden Staatskapelle would have been an opportunity for Kempe to work intensively again in opera, something he had rarely done in recent years. On the few occasions when he had agreed to conduct an opera, his forebodings about rehearsal and ensemble misery were reinforced. Now a new source of aggravation was added: 'we seem to be living in an age when producers behave as though it's always carnival time. The crimes these people are committing against music are beyond the bounds of tolerance'—and Kempe's tolerance was far-reaching. In a production of *Salome* in the Roman amphitheatre at Orange, the antics of two hundred or so extras drawn from the Foreign Legion totally ruined the orchestral postlude which follows the dialogue between Salome and Jokanaan. The palace guards, who had been dreamed up by the producer together with a horde of beggars surrounding Jokanaan, were told to drive the beggars off with violent lashings of their whips. At this point Kempe put down his baton and left the conductor's desk: 'For this circus I need other music.' Very different was the occasion when, before a full cast for *Zigeunerbaron*, Walter Felsenstein had had the generosity to admit to the then young Kempe that as producer he had miscalculated a tempo, and immediately altered his staging accordingly. 'Those days are long past!' Only in Covent Garden Kempe still enjoyed making opera. 'This house has kept its ensemble spirit, and there is musical respect and understanding. There one can simply give one's all to the music.'

In fact there was another reason why Rudolf Kempe withdrew more and more from opera and from the commitment he had felt musically to certain scores in earlier days. 'The perversity of the *Salome* plot makes me sick now. And not even the beautiful music of the recognition scene between Elektra and Orestes can compensate for that horrible scream from Elektra—"Triff noch einmal!" when Klytemnestra is murdered. If I think it over seriously, I feel for the same reason I couldn't conduct either *Otello* or *Butterfly* again. And what is left of Wagner's for me? *Meistersinger* of course, at most *Parsifal*, *Tristan* and maybe some bits from *Valkyrie*. The rest I can't bear any more.'

Kempe's gentle sensitivity, strained to the point of exhaustion by the events of the war—and not only by them—had brought him to this state of revulsion from violence. However, it was his very sensitivity, perhaps the most meaningful part of his nature, that made him what he was—a conductor with the ability literally to listen, and with a readiness to adjust entirely to those with whom he made music. In particular singers, who might ruin their voices by trying not to be drowned in waves of orchestral sound, were grateful to him for the subtle way he graded his dynamics, especially in heavily scored operas by Strauss and Wagner. They also benefited from the freedom in tempo he gave them to breathe and phrase, in the same way that orchestral players benefited from his awareness that chords in the different sections of strings, wind and brass need different periods of time to speak. Such technical or intellectual problems did not prevent Kempe from becoming deeply involved emotionally in opera. How much feeling he drew from the text could never go unnoticed by anyone who heard him conduct *Rosenkavalier*, *The Magic Flute*, *Meistersinger*, *Bohème* or *Falstaff*. For all his mental and physical command and control he was by nature a purely emotional man. Occasionally he was wrongly judged as being too controlled, as being 'a conductor of coolly dosed and calculated emotion'. Such misjudgements were perhaps due to the exclusivity with which his feelings, never worn on his shirt sleeve, found their way directly into music through the natural yet never superficial elegance of his gestures. Every move was meaningful, nothing was superfluous. The sincerity of his feelings gave his music-making that power of expression which, in spite of all variations in individual taste, makes an interpretation valid and acceptable the very moment it is presented. Kempe's power of expression was based on his outlook: 'One must not search, one must find. Searching implies conscious manipulation; finding is the result of devotion to a composer and his music.'

Whenever Kempe met again on the concert platform singers like Janet Baker, Dietrich Fischer-Dieskau or Heather Harper, Anna Reynolds, Theo Adam or Yvonne Minton, their pleasure showed how much they missed him in opera. To balance this, of course, instrumentalists now benefited from his withdrawal from the opera house. At all times Kempe greatly enjoyed accompanying. He displayed an understanding which accepted interpretations even though they differed from his own ideas. The more unpredictably a soloist would change his tempo, the more Kempe seemed to relish partnering him. An example is Cherkassky, who used to give a concert performance totally different from the one he had rehearsed, and could zig-zag any way his fancy took him—Kempe was always with him. 'To accompany needs only a little anticipation of what a partner is going to do, and a little stick technique.' Only to a soloist whose eccentricity bounded on the pathological would he point out, discreetly but firmly, that, for instance, the piano concerto he was playing was originally composed by Robert Schumann.

Alongside the established figures in music—soloists like Serkin, Rubinstein, Curzon, Kempff, Menuhin, Clara Haskil, David Oistrakh, Szeryng, Schneiderhan, Rostal, Fournier, Zara Nelsova and Tortelier—it was the young generation that he liked to perform with. Pianists of the calibre of Malcolm Frager, Radu Lupu, Bruno

Gelber, Nelson Freire, Ilana Vered, Garrick Ohlsson and Nerine Barrett, and violinists such as Itzhak Pearlman, Gidon Kremer, Edith Peinemann, Ulf Hoelscher, Miriam Fried, Teiko Maehashi and Kyung-wha Chung, often featured in his programmes, as did the young 'cellists Esther Nyffenegger and Angelica May. What impressed Kempe more than technical perfection—'this has nowadays to be taken for granted anyhow'—or lists of reviews and awards, was a player's personal style, if it went hand in glove with the composition. If the ideas of personalising a score were not quite convincing, Kempe would advise with infinite patience, often without the young musicians even being aware of what he was doing. 'The isolated life of a soloist forces them to give solo recitals night after night, or play concertos with often only one orchestra rehearsal. This is why their feeling of togetherness in performance is sometimes not fully developed.' With a conductor like Kempe togetherness of ensemble became infectious. Rudolf Serkin says of him, 'Whatever he makes is chamber music.' And the only thing Kempe would never tolerate was an attitude which refused to make music as part of an ensemble—for him, this was not a question of being able, but of being willing.

Kempe himself would grasp any opportunity to sit at the keyboard and actually play chamber music. 'Of course I am no pianist' (this was something of an understatement), 'but when I am playing myself at least I know what to expect, and this is a comforting feeling.' The Chemnitz days when he had treated a greedy audience to three of the biggest concertos in one programme (Schumann, Beethoven's Fifth and Tchaikovsky's First), all played on two pianos with a colleague to accompany him—those days were long past. And to play concertos with an orchestra, as he had frequently done in Dresden as Music Director with the Kapelle, he now had neither time nor nerves for. However, his technique was still quite remarkable, considering he had so little time for practice. Whenever he joined his orchestra musicians in concerts to perform sonatas, piano quintets or his favourite piece, Wolf-Ferrari's *Kammersinfonie*, or when he accompanied Brahms or Wolf lieder, the question whether he was a pianist or not became irrelevant. And when in a Mozart piano trio he played the melody in the slow movement, he made the listeners forget everything—and the string players, nearly, their entrances.

Bach's concertos for two harpsichords, performed with another Dresdener, Karl Richter, became a typically Saxon affair, and not only musically. Despite their often successful efforts to speak 'high German', they inevitably resorted to unmistakable dialect when one played a wrong note and the other tried to assuage his colleague's zeal for perfection by shouting 'The Gods demand retribution!' This mania for perfection used to befall Kempe whenever he was playing himself. Regarding other musicians, his opinion was, 'There are actually no right or wrong notes—just musical or unmusical ones.'

In this respect, Kempe's Munich colleagues, Rafael Kubelik and Fritz Rieger, entirely agreed with him when he invited them to join him for a Munich Philharmonic concert performance of Bach's Triple Keyboard Concerto. The harmony between the three players was so exceptional that Kubelik at once retaliated by inviting them, together with Wolfgang Sawallisch, to perform for Bavarian Radio and Television Bach's transcription of the Vivaldi Concerto for four harpsichords. Happily, Bach left it at four keyboards; it might have been difficult to find more conductors ready to join their colleagues to make music together....

If on these occasions, Kempe always chose the least prominent keyboard, it was a sign of his proverbial modesty, exemplified by his fondness for spaghetti and tomato sauce and by his firm refusal to wear 'frippery' as he would call patent leather shoes or rings and gold wrist watches. It also showed itself in his habit of mishearing any form of address except that of 'Mr. Kempe', and in his open disregard for medals or titles or any kind of fuss made over him. It culminated in his total inability to speak of himself. If after a concert someone would congratulate him on a great performance, he would reply with a smile, 'It is a beautiful symphony, isn't it? And didn't the orchestra play splendidly tonight?' However, if anything failed to come up to his standard, then it was hard to convince him it was not his fault. A term like 'success', which—and not only from artists—can be heard over and over again like a cracked record, would never have passed his lips—not even to the person closest to him, from whom he would never conceal any weakness. Thank goodness, he had a fair number of them, and they were possibly the most lovable part of his nature.

Even in non-musical matters Kempe earned confidence because of the way he respected the individual in every person he met, be it a taxi driver or the Queen of England. His quiet, friendly attitude—never condescending and never aloof—showed itself to everyone, and beneath a veneer of detachment one could sense his warmth and readiness to help, a readiness which made it easy for people, not only musicians, to seek his counsel without denting their self-respect. He had too an enviable rapport with young people: his natural open-mindedness, shown to young musicians and children alike in the way he would take them seriously, evoked a mixture of respect and trust which made nonsense of the so-called generation gap.

His concern for musical recruits, derived from both professional and human understanding, manifested itself among other ways in his support of the English 'Rehearsal

Orchestra' of which he was patron for many years. This institution offers opportunities to young musicians entering the profession to gain what is not taught in academies—orchestral experience and practical training covering the entire opera and concert repertoire, passed on by experienced musicians and instrumentalists. Kempe derived great satisfaction in working with this orchestra and would gladly have spent more time with them if it had been available. 'The idea of this orchestra is magnificent, and we need it desperately. Until it catches on elsewhere, particularly on the Continent, the standard of orchestral recruits cannot be raised.'

Another problem which Kempe had at heart was the training of conductors, a problem which troubled him more and more in later years. 'Young people often make the basic mistake of believing that playing a gramophone record at home and contorting themselves with impressive gestures in front of a mirror is all they need to do to be appointed as Chief Conductor of some orchestra or other, the following day. Sadly, this does happen sometimes and, when it does, all concerned have to pay for it. Every musician must practise his instrument in the first place, and a conductor's instrument is the orchestra. To hang around waiting for a chance to conduct one concert in two seasons is a sheer waste of time'. Kempe's advice, to study the piano properly, to play full scores and to learn the trade by coaching in an opera house, wasn't always received with understanding and enthusiasm. It happened more than once, when Kempe gave young conductors a chance to conduct a concert or a rehearsal with one of his orchestras, that their lack of understanding made itself evident in a most embarrassing way.

Whenever he could spare some time during the last years he gave conducting lessons, and there was little of the academic about them. Apart from conducting technique, he imparted to his students invaluable advice from his experience in orchestra psychology, without ever calling it that. This experience proved itself even more in rehearsals (and attending these was far more useful anyhow in Kempe's opinion than having lessons). Indeed Kempe himself was a living proof that there is no need to have made a life-study of psychology in order to come to terms with people. For instance, it was almost impossible to quarrel with a man like him; the very few who succeeded in doing so must have had a special talent that way. No musician ever heard Kempe speak with a raised voice, and if he had a bone to pick with somebody he would never do so in front of an orchestra. If anybody came to him to apologise for something he would only shake his head: 'I haven't the slightest idea what you're talking about.' And if it happened that, after a good first-night performance, some avoidable mishap marred the second night, Kempe would call the musicians together before the third performance. Feeling somewhat responsible, they would expect the due reproach. 'Gentlemen, as far as I can recall there was an excellent performance last Friday. Tonight, I think we are going to have another!' It would be even better.

'Duty above all' was one of Kempe's mottoes. In German, 'duty' is used to cover any kind of musical session work, and on the lips of orchestral veterans—even thirty years before they retire—the bureaucratic ring of this word can smash any form of musical idealism. However, when Kempe spoke about duty, it sounded quite different. The word only had an ominous ring when he was prevented from fulfilling his duty—if his studies were interrupted or his rest was disturbed in the afternoon before a concert, or something delayed his arrival in good time for a performance. In such cases Kempe could be abrupt to the point of being impolite.

However, he relaxed in a way that, again, might have been taken as impolite as soon as duty was done. The alacrity with which he cast off his tails, beginning at the doorstep of his house, the zany habit of decorating lamps and music stands with discarded socks, and above all the absurdity of his comments on even more absurd television programmes—all this was a means of relaxing, and was certainly one of the secrets behind his power of concentration. 'If you haven't got the courage to let your hair down, you can't renew your energy.' In this Kempe was a master. With uncanny assurance he knew how to pace himself and others in rehearsal and concert conditions, how to regain strength and how to be sparing in its expenditure when necessary. His finely judged tempi and the balance of his transitions, convincing in their naturalness whether in a Bruckner symphony or a Puccini opera, were a hallmark of all that he did, in music and elsewhere. His spare-time occupations ranged from doing absolutely nothing (except 'philosophising about nothing') or undertaking do-it-yourself jobs, to intense involvement with serious subjects. On holiday he would sometimes spend sixteen hours a day gazing at the sea and talking 'rubbish', or with a racquet in his hand, and a mischievous grin on his face, he would chase a compliant victim around the tennis court; at home he would design and construct complex model railway circuits worthy of a professional engineer. And sometimes, escaping from everything, he immersed himself in astronomy. Whatever he did was done with a sense of form and order, precise yet never pedantic, and with a loving care and patient tenderness which are the very secret of a 'golden hand'.

Kempe's belief that relaxation is a vital element in music as well as in the everyday life of an orchestra was put into practice whenever he had an opportunity. The concerts of light music which he occasionally gave during the last years in London, Zurich, Dresden, and especially in Munich at carnival time with the Philharmonic, served to relax taut nerves in public and orchestra alike. No one who missed these concerts would have imagined how high-spirited Kempe could be as he introduced the items or played pop songs on the accordeon or performed the solo on the cuckoo pipe in Johann Strauss the younger's *Krapfenwaldl Polka*. It was hard to believe that an interpreter of Bruckner's symphonies like Kempe could also present hits from musicals and other frivolities with such impish glee and verve (it clearly looked back to his days in the Bad Schandau café). His old admiration for Karl Valentin, the cabaret comedian, was reflected in the deadly seriousness with which Kempe, in the grey uniform of an orchestral librarian, would carefully put out the music parts on the wrong desks. Above all he enjoyed parodying avant-garde piano music, and poking fun at his own well-known aversion to it: to a metronomic percussion accompaniment, he brushed his hair and the strings of a grand piano with a lavatory brush, then dashed off the most amazing virtuoso keyboard passages with the utmost precision while wearing woolly mittens; and just as precise was the timing of his sprints round the piano in silent bars. Kempe's *Violin Concerto to End All Violin Concertos*, like several other of his arrangements, would have aroused even Gerard Hoffnung's envy. It includes almost every well-known tune and all the most difficult passages from the popular concertos, ranging from Mozart to Tchaikovsky, in the original orchestration. Interrupted by apparently endless virtuoso cadenzas, the quotations are seamlessly woven into one another with such skill, and alternate at such prodigious speed, that even experts find it hard to tell where Brahms ends and Dvořák begins.

Whatever 'happenings' Kempe concocted for these programmes—called 'Philharmonic off the Rails'—never descended to vulgarity or bad taste, whether he were flirting with ladies in the choir or eating doughnuts while conducting the *Krapfenwaldl (Doughnut) Polka*. His sense of humour was infectious, and, being aware that in this field it is always more blessed to receive than to give, he never gave hurt or offence. The warmth of his humour went straight to everyone's heart.

Time and again in his last years Rudolf Kempe would pause for breath, looking back as people sometimes do who have faced death and so take nothing as a matter of course except the truth that 'all flows past'. At such moments he would say, 'It has all happened by chance; things came to me, so I accepted them—no more.' If anything filled him with grateful pride it was the fact that throughout his career he had never had to grasp. And thus he had felt neither hatred nor envy. His humble upbringing he would never deny; his noble mind and generous heart may have shamed others who considered themselves superior by birth or education. His qualities as an artist, and what he achieved through those qualities, were never taken by him as a personal merit; his work was the unquestionable tribute he paid in return for his inborn gifts. Early in life he had learned to do without many things which others might regard as their due, and so he accepted with a constantly renewed gratitude even the smallest things as gifts of life. Before them he blossomed with a child-like awe and wonder which epitomised his youthful charm and open-mindedness. This open-mindedness, however, made him vulnerable. Unconsciously he often tried to mask this vulnerability and thus appeared more reserved than in reality he was. Only late in life did he realise that his unshielded nature needed no protection; it was his very strength, for it came from the same source as his assurance and composure, the cheerfulness and peace of mind he gave to others—from his humility.

Had he ever wanted to put this into words, perhaps he would have chosen those from *Der Rosenkavalier*:

> '... It's all a mystery, so deep a mystery.
> And one is here to endure it.
> And in the "how", there lies the whole difference....'

Munich, 1970 ▷

Following pages: *Rehearsals with the Munich Philharmonic (1971)*

Rehearsing Richard Strauss's 'Alpine Symphony' with the Dresden Staatskapelle for record and concert, 1971

After a successful 'Alpine excursion': Playback with recording producers David Mottley, E.M.I. (front), and Heinz Wegner, Eterna (on Kempe's left)

In holiday mood: an unbeatable technique!

If it's raining—at home, a tape recording of 'the Avantgardist' (by playback technique the entire 'kitchen-department' is operated single-handed!)

A Munich Philharmonic concert in the Herkulessaal of the Munich Residenz (1972)

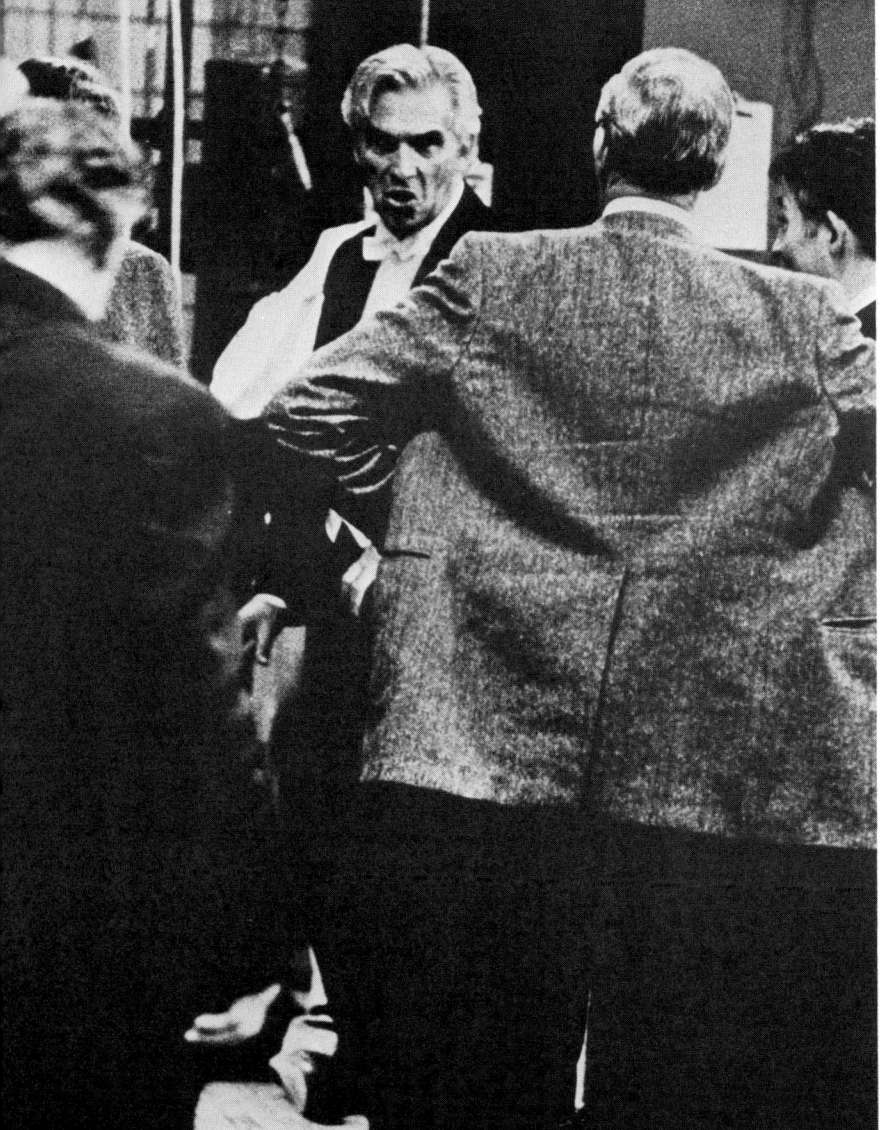

THE 'ROYAL PHIL'S' AMERICAN TOUR IN 1972

Having some fresh air—with daughters Ina and Karin

Short break on the highway

◁ *'Must I really go to this party??!!'*

Next page:

Keep smiling—with principal viola Fred Riddle and violin soloist Teiko Maehashi

Dialogue with the principal 'cello

The opening concert of the 1972/73 Carnegie Hall season in New York

Four Munich conductors join together for a performance of Bach/Vivaldi's A minor Concerto: with Fritz Rieger, Rafael Kubelik and Wolfgang Sawallisch in the Herkulessaal, November 1972

A trio recital with the Munich Philharmonic's principal 'cello, Fritz Kiskalt, in Zurich, 1974

New Year's Eve in Dresden with 'the Kapelle': 'Flederkavalier'—or 'Rosenmaus'?

Rehearsal for the New Year's Eve 1972/73 concert in the Dresden Theatre: Léhar's 'Gold and Silver' waltz

Recording sessions in the Munich Bürgerbräu brewery hall, June 1973: Beethoven's Choral Symphony with the Munich Philharmonic Orchestra, the Philharmonic and Motette Choirs; soloists (from right to left) Ursula Koszut, Brigitte Fassbaender, Nicolai Gedda and Donald MacIntyre

RECORDING BRAHMS'S B FLAT MAJOR CONCERTO WITH BRUNO LEONARDO GELBER AND THE 'ROYAL PHIL', IN LONDON, SEPTEMBER 1973

Playback: '--- any problems?'

'Not for us!'

'Any further complaints from the technical side?'   'Well done!'

AT HOME

A new model train

Snapshots

—not quite happy with the results?

In between—correspondence

Conducting the Rehearsal Orchestra in Bishopsgate Institute, London, 1974
Advice for the young Leader

...*and back to the 'Dresdeners': recording—*

—and results: 'For me it's good enough...'

FESTIVAL D'ORANGE

The Roman amphitheatre

'Salome', 1974:
Rehearsal with Leonie Rysanek
(standing), Marga Schiml and
Horst Laubenthal

'VALKYRIE', 1975: Rehearsal—

—and intermezzo: Reunion of two fellow-countrymen (Theo Adam, Wotan)

The Munich Philharmonic's Russian tour in 1974: Bruckner's Fifth Symphony in the Leningrad Philharmonic Hall

The Chairman presents as a souvenir a sketch of Arturo Toscanini by Fjodor Chaliapin
THE ROYAL PHILHARMONIC'S FAREWELL PARTY, JULY 1975

Chairman and General Manager

Public Relations Manager

'AUF WIEDERSEHEN' TO ALL OF THEM—

The longest-serving member

Principal 'cello
and—last but not least—the orchestra porters

Rehearsal in the Royal Albert Hall

NEW YET OLD FRIENDS: THE B.B.C. SYMPHONY ORCHESTRA

...as one wind player to another...

Dvořák's 'New World' in a Prom concert in the Albert Hall, August 1975

General rehearsal with 'the' Dresden Orchestra, January 1976: Stravinsky's 'Firebird'

A Dresden concert

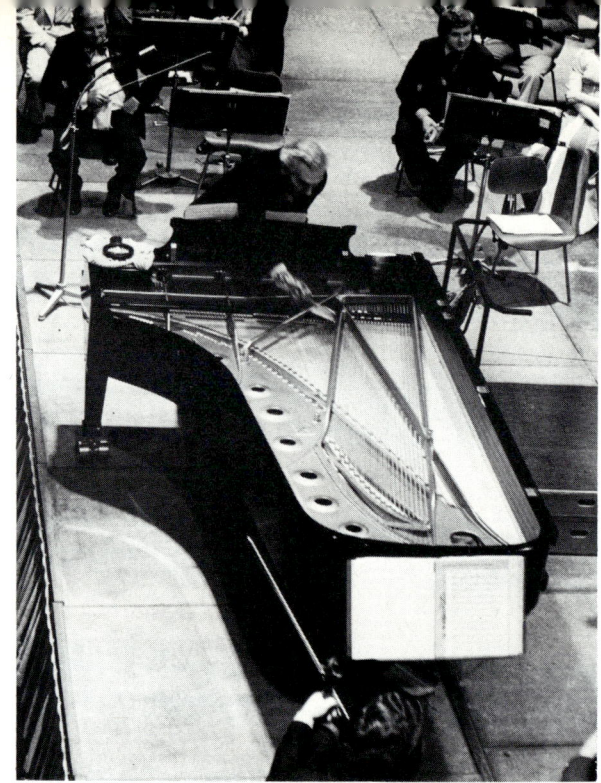

'Das kann doch einen Seemann nicht...' (sea shanty)

Demonstrating his love of modern music

THE MUNICH PHIL AND THEIR CHIEF CONDUCTOR 'OFF THE RAILS'—CARNIVAL CONCERTS 1976

The Munich Philharmonic competing against the Fire Brigade Band of Disharmoning

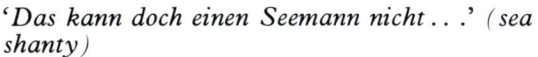

Solo cuckoo in J. Strauss's 'Krapfenwaldl Polka'

Flirting with 'Fair Lady' June Card

Final applause

At home at the harpsichord

Discography
Compiled by Charles Blyth and Denham Ford

KEY

A Guide to the Prefixes and Abbreviations used in the Kempe Discography

Acanta	German label which took over the short-lived BASF label in 1977	HQS	EMI stereo reissues (England)
		KBACC	BASF cassette prefix
Advent	Cassette label (U.S.)	Kr.	Kristall—EMI reissue label (Germany)
ALP	EMI mono original releases (England)	KSXC	Decca cassette prefix (England)
Ang	Angel	Lon	London (U.S.)
ARK	RCA cassette prefix (England)	MFP	EMI mono reissues; 'Music for Pleasure' (England)
ASD	EMI stereo original releases (England)	MPS	Musikproduction Schwarzwald (Germany)
BASF	See Acanta	Parl	Parliament
BLP	EMI mono 10" original releases (England)	Pick	Pickwick (U.S.)
C	See '1C 000-00 000' below	Quint.	Quintessence (U.S.)
Cap	Capitol (U.S.)	RD	Reader's Digest, individual record numbers from sets; RCA productions
CBS	Affiliates of Columbia in England and Germany		
CFP	EMI stereo reissues; 'Classics for Pleasure' (England)	Sera	Seraphim (U.S.)
Col	Columbia (U.S.)	SHZEL	EMI reissue label (Germany)
Conn	Connoisseur Society (U.S.)	SLS	EMI stereo sets (England)
DaCa	Da Camera (Germany)	Supra	Supraphone (Czechoslovakian)
Dec	Decca (England and Germany)	SXDW	EMI; HMV stereo set (England)
DF	Prefix of German Acanta and BASF cassettes	SXLP	EMI stereo reissues; 'HMV Concert Classics' (England)
Elec	Electrola; designates earlier mono and stereo EMI releases in Germany	TC	EMI cassette prefix (England)
		Tel	Teldec (Germany)
EMB	Reissue label of CBS (England)	Tud	Tudor (Zurich, Switzerland)
ESD	EMI stereo reissues; 'Greensleeves' (England)	Ultra	Ultraphone (Czechoslovakian)
Eterna	Classics label of VEB Deutsche Schallplatten (East Germany)	WRC	EMI; reissues; 'World Record Club' (England)
Euro	Ariola-Eurodisc (Germany)	XLP	EMI mono reissues; 'HMV Concert Classics' (England)
GK	RCA cassette prefix (England)		
HMV	EMI; 'His Master's Voice' (England)	ZCWR	WRC cassette prefix (England)
HQM	EMI mono reissues (England)		

1C 000-00 000   Standard form of later European EMI releases. The '1' preceding the 'C' signifies Germany. French and Italian releases (not included in this discography) have '2' and '3' respectively

4XG   Prefix of Seraphim cassettes

FORMAT

COMPOSER NAME
Title of Work
    Orchestra Name;   (Year recorded)   [G] = Germany
    Soloists; Choral group   [E] = England
        [A] = America

	Mono Record Nos.	Stereo/Quad Nos.	Cassettes
1. First recording of two or more.			
2. Second recording, etc.	10" & 12" LPs; The unique 45 rpm & 78 rpm discs are footnoted.	12" Stereo discs; Quad recordings signified by (Q) after the number.	
> Signifies reference to the larger work or more complete recording listed directly above.			

Composer / Work / Collaborating Artists	Mono Recordings	Stereo / Quad Recordings	Cassettes
BACH, JOHANN SEBASTIAN Suite No. 3 in D Berlin Philharmonic	(1956) [G] Elec E 80018		

Composer / Work / Collaborating Artists	Mono Recordings	Stereo / Quad Recordings	Cassettes
BAYER, JOSEF Die Puppenfee: Ballet Music Vienna Philharmonic	(1961) [E] ALP 1974	[E] ASD 525 SXLP 30083	
BEETHOVEN, LUDWIG VAN Piano Concerto No. 5 in E-Flat, Op. 73 1. Berlin Philharmonic; Jakob Gimpel, pf.	(1957) [G] Elec E 80025 [E] XLP 20004	[G] Elec STE 80025 [E] SXLP 20004 [A] Genesis GS 1002	
2. Royal Philharmonic; Rudolf Firkusny, pf.	(1964)	[E] RCA GL 25014 [A] RD 4-60-1	[E] GK 25014
Coriolan Overture, Op. 62 Berlin Philharmonic	(1956/57) [G] Elec E 80029 [E] ALP 1663 MFP 2056 [A] Cap G 7140	[G] Elec STE 80029 Kr. SMVP 8037 1C 047-50 513 [E] ASD 336 [A] Cap SG 7140 Cap SP 8635	
Egmont Overture, Op. 84 1. Berlin Philharmonic	(1956/57) [G] Elec E 80029 [E] ALP 1663 MFP 2056 [A] Cap G 7140	[G] Elec STE 80029 Kr. SMVP 8037 1C 047-50 513 [E] ASD 336 [A] Cap SG 7140 Cap SP 8635	
2. Munich Philharmonic	(1971)	[G] in 1C 147-02 506/13 (Q) 1C 051-02 509 (Q) [E] in SLS 892 (Q) [A] in Sera SIH 6093 (Q)	[G] 1C 225-02 509
Fidelio Overture Berlin Philharmonic	(1956/57) [G] Elec E 80029 [E] ALP 1663 MFP 2056 [A] Cap G 7140	[G] Elec STE 80029 Kr. SMVP 8037 1C 047-50 513 [E] ASD 336 [A] Cap SG 7140 Cap SP 8635	
Leonore Overture No. 3 1. Berlin Philharmonic	(1956/57) [G] Elec E 80029 [E] ALP 1663 MFP 2056 [A] Cap G 7140	[G] Elec STE 80029 Kr. SMVP 8037 1C 047-50 513 [E] ASD 336 [A] Cap SG 7140 Cap SP 8635	
2. Munich Philharmonic	(1971/73)	[G] in 1C 147-02 506/13(Q) 1C 037-02 508(Q) [E] in SLS 892(Q) [A] in Sera SIH 6093(Q)	[G] 1C 237-02 508
Prometheus Overture, Op. 43 1. Berlin Philharmonic	(1956/57) [G] Elec E 80029 [E] ALP 1663 MFP 2056	[G] Elec STE 80029 Kr. SMVP 8037 1C 047-50 513 [E] ASD 336	

Composer / Work / Collaborating Artists	Mono Recordings	Stereo / Quad Recordings	Cassettes
BEETHOVEN, LUDWIG VAN (cont.)			
	[A] Cap G 7140	[A] Cap SG 7140 Cap SP 8635	
2. Munich Philharmonic (1971)		[G] in 1C 147-02 506/13(Q) 1C 051-02 507(Q) [E] in SLS 892(Q) [A] in Sera SIH 6093(Q)	[G] 1C 225-02 507
Symphony No. 1 in C, Op. 21 Munich Philharmonic (1971/73)		[G] in 1C 147-02 506/13(Q) 1C 037-02 883(Q) [E] in SLS 892(Q) [A] in Sera SIH 6093(Q)	[G] 1C 237-02 883
Symphony No. 2 in D, Op. 36 Munich Philharmonic (1971/73)		[G] in 1C 147-02 506/13(Q) [E] in SLS 892(Q) [A] in Sera SIH 6093(Q)	
Symphony No. 3 in E-Flat, Op. 55 1. Berlin Philharmonic (1959)		[G] Elec STE 80535 Kr. SMVP 8004 1C 047-50 507	
	[E] ALP 1854	[E] ASD 426 WRC ST 942	
	[A] Cap L 9218	[A] Cap SL 9218	
2. Munich Philharmonic (1971)		[G] in 1C 147-02 506/13(Q) 1C 051-02 507(Q) [E] in SLS 892(Q) [A] in Sera SIH 6093(Q)	[G] 1C 225-02 507
Symphony No. 4 in B-Flat, Op. 60 Munich Philharmonic (1971/73)		[G] in 1C 147-02 506/13(Q) 1C 037-02 508(Q) [E] in SLS 892(Q) [A] in Sera SIH 6093(Q)	[G] 1C 237-02 508
Symphony No. 5 in C Minor, Op. 67 1. Munich Philharmonic (1971)		[G] in 1C 147-02 506/13(Q) 1C 051-02 509(Q) [E] in SLS 892(Q) [A] in Sera SIH 6093(Q)	[G] 1C 225-02 509
2. Zurich Tonhalle (1972)		Tud. 73001 (Swiss)	Tud. 73501
Symphony No. 6 in F, Op. 68 Munich Philharmonic (1972)		[G] in 1C 147-02 506/13(Q) 1C 051-02 510(Q) [E] in SLS 892(Q) ESD 7004(Q) [A] in Sera SIH 6093(Q)	[G] 1C 225-02 510 [E] TC ESD 7004
Symphony No. 7 in A, Op. 92 Munich Philharmonic (1971)		[G] in 1C 147-02 506/13(Q) 1C 037-02 511(Q) [E] in SLS 892(Q) [A] in Sera SIH 6093(Q)	[G] 1C 237-02 511
Symphony No. 8 in F, Op. 93 Munich Philharmonic (1971/73)		[G] in 1C 147-02 506/13(Q) 1C 037-02 883(Q) [E] in SLS 892(Q) [A] in Sera SIH 6093(Q)	[G] 1C 237-02 883

Composer / Work / Collaborating Artists		Mono Recordings	Stereo / Quad Recordings	Cassettes
Symphony No. 9 in D Minor, Op. 125 Munich Philharmonic; Ursula Koszut, Brigitte Fassbänder, Nicolai Gedda, Donald McIntyre; Munich Philharmonic Choir and Munich Motet Choir	(1971/73)		[G] in 1C 147-02 506/13(Q) 1C 145-02 761/62(Q) [E] in SLS 892(Q) [A] in Sera SIH 6093(Q)	
BERLIOZ, HECTOR				
Roman Carnival Overture, Op. 9 Vienna Philharmonic	(1958)	[E] ALP 1765 XLP 30077	[G] Kr. SMVP 8061 [E] ASD 330 SXLP 30077	
Symphonie Fantastique, Op. 14 Berlin Philharmonic	(1959)	[G] Elec E 80491 [E] XLP 20088	[G] Elec STE 80491 1C 051-03 013 [E] SXLP 20088	[G] 1C 225-03 013
BIZET, GEORGES				
L'Arlésienne Suites 1 and 2 Bamberg Symphony	(1963)	[G] Euro 70794 KK [E] Oriole RM 200 Oriole RM 52200	[G] Euro S 70795 KK Euro 88705 XAK	[G] Euro 55482 VK
BRAHMS, JOHANNES				
Piano Concerto No. 1 in D Minor, Op. 15 Berlin Philharmonic; Jakob Gimpel, pf.	(1958)	[G] Elec E 80427 [E] XLP 20010	[G] Elec STE 80427 [E] SXLP 20010	
Piano Concerto No. 2 in B-Flat, Op. 83 Royal Philharmonic; Bruno Leonardo-Gelber, pf.	(1973)		[G] 1C 063-12 788(Q) [E] in SXDW 3020 [A] Conn. CSQ 2088(Q)	[G] 1C 243-12 788 [A] Advent E-1053
Violin Concerto in D, Op. 77 Berlin Philharmonic; Yehudi Menuhin, v.	(1957)	[G] Elec E 90017 [E] ALP 1568 [A] Cap PAO 8410	[G] Elec STE 90017 Elec SME 90017 SHZEL 716 [E] ASD 264 SXLP 30186 [A] Cap SG 7173	
A German Requiem, Op. 45 Berlin Philharmonic; Elisabeth Grümmer, Dietrich Fischer-Dieskau; St Hedwig's Cathedral Choir	(1955)	[G] Elec E 90003/04S [E] ALPS 1351 and ALP 1352 XLP 30073/74	[G] 1C 147-28 550/51 (r)	
Tragic Overture, Op. 81 Berlin Philharmonic	(1960)	[E] ALP 1824	[G] Elec STE 80582 [E] ASD 406 SXLP 30100	
'Haydn' Variations, Op. 56a				
1. Berlin Philharmonic	(1956)	[G] Elec E 80018		
2. Bamberg Symphony	(1963)	[G] Euro 70470 KK [E] Oriole RM 201 Oriole RM 52201 WRC T 437	[G] Euro S 70471 KK Euro 27641 XAK	
3. Munich Philharmonic	(1975)		[G] BASF 20 223930 in Acanta JB 23033 Acanta DC 22393	[G] DF 323930 DF 32393

Composer / Work / Collaborating Artists		Mono Recordings	Stereo / Quad Recordings	Cassettes
BRAHMS, JOHANNES (cont.)				
Symphony No. 1 in C Minor, Op. 68				
1. Berlin Philharmonic	(1959)	[G] Elec E 80459	[G] Elec STE 80459	
			1C 047-50 538	
		[E] ALP 1772	[E] ASD 350	
		MFP 2012	CFP 131	
		[A] Cap G 7208	[A] Cap SG 7208	
2. Munich Philharmonic	(1975)		[G] BASF 20 223914	[G] DF 323914
			in Acanta JB 23033	
			Acanta DC 22391	
			Acanta DF 32391	
			[E] BASF BAC 3083	
Symphony No. 2 in D, Op. 73				
1. Berlin Philharmonic	(1955)	[G] Elec E 80004		
		[E] ALP 1386		
		XLP 30043		
2. Bamberg Symphony	(1963)	[G] Euro 70610 KK	[G] Euro S 70611 KK	
			Euro 27641 XAK	
		[E] WRC T 424		
3. Munich Philharmonic	(1975)		[G] BASF DC 223922	
			in Acanta JB 23033	
			Acanta DC 22302	[G] DF 32502
Symphony No. 3 in F, Op. 90				
1. Berlin Philharmonic	(1960)		[G] Elec STE 80582	
		[E] ALP 1824	[E] ASD 406	
			SXLP 30100	
2. Munich Philharmonic	(1975)		[G] BASF 20 223930	[G] DF 323930
			in Acanta JB 23033	
			Acanta DC 22393	[G] DF 32393
Symphony No. 4 in E Minor, Op. 98				
1. Berlin Philharmonic	(1956)	[G] Elec E 80017		
		[E] ALP 1545		
		[A] Cap G 7100		
2. Royal Philharmonic	(1960)		[G] 1C 047-50 800	
		[E] ALP 1894	[E] ASD 461	
			WRC ST 932	
3. Munich Philharmonic	(1975)		[G] BASF 20 223949	[G] DF 323949
			in Acanta JB 23033	
			Acanta DC 22394	[G] DF 32394
			[E] BASF BAC 3064	[E] KBACC 3064
BRITTEN, BENJAMIN				
Sinfonia da Requiem, Op. 20				
Staatskapelle Dresden	(1976)		[G] Eterna 827 012	
			(East Germany)	
BRUCH, MAX				
Violin Concerto No. 1 in G Minor, Op. 26				
Royal Philharmonic; Kyung-Wha Chung, v.	(1972)		[G] Dec SXL 6573	[G] 4.41483 CX
			Tel 6.41483 AW	
			[E] Dec SXL 6573	[E] KSXC 6573
			[A] Lon CS 6795	
Scottish Fantasy, Op. 46				
Royal Philharmonic; Kyung-Wha Chung, v.	(1972)		[G] Dec SXL 6573	[G] 4.41483 CX
			Tel 6.41483 AW	
			[E] Dec SXL 6573	[E] KSXC 6573
			[A] Lon CS 6795	

Composer / Work / Collaborating Artists		Mono Recordings	Stereo / Quad Recordings	Cassettes
BRUCKNER, ANTON				
Symphony No. 4 in E-Flat				
Munich Philharmonic	(1975)		[G] BASF EB 227391	
			Acanta EB 22739	
Symphony No. 5 in B-Flat				
Munich Philharmonic	(1974)		[G] BASF 39 22526/27	
			Acanta HA 22526	
Symphony No. 8 in C Minor (1890 version)				
Zurich Tonhalle	(1973)		Tud 74003/04(Q) (Swiss)	Tud 74503/04
CHOPIN, FREDERIC				
Piano Concerto No. 2 in F Minor, Op. 21				
Royal Philharmonic; Shura Cherkassy, pf.	(1966)		[A] RD 4-41-4	
DVORAK, ANTONIN				
Rusalka: 'Song to the Moon' (in German)				
Berlin Philharmonic; Elisabeth Lindermeier, s.	(1957)	[G] Elec E 80027		
Scherzo capriccioso in D-Flat, Op. 66				
1. Berlin Philharmonic	(1957)	[G] Elec E 80027		
2. Royal Philharmonic	(1961)	[E] ALP 1880	[E] ASD 449	
			SXLP 30110	
			SXLP 30125	
			[A] Sera S 60098	
Serenade for Strings in E, Op. 22				
Munich Philharmonic	(1968)		[G] CBS S 72711	
			[E] in CBS 78210	
			CBS 61811	[E] CBS 40 61811
Symphony No. 8 in G, Op. 88				
Munich Philharmonic	(1972)		[G] in BASF 29 21770-1	
			in MPS 88009	
Symphony No. 9 in E Minor, Op. 95				
1. Berlin Philharmonic	(1957)	[G] Elec E 80026	[G] Elec STE 80026	
			Kr. SMVP 8015	
			1C 047-50 508	
		[E] ALP 1623	[E] ASD 380	
			SXLP 30110	
2. Royal Philharmonic	(1963)		[A] RD 4-2-13	
3. Zurich Tonhalle	(1972)		Tud 73002 (Swiss)	Tud 73502
GLIERE, REINHOLD				
Harp Concerto in E-Flat, Op. 74				
Leipzig Philharmonic; Zutta Joff, h.		[A] Urania 7164	[A] Urania 57164 (r)	
GLUCK, CHRISTOPH WILLIBALD				
Ballet Suite (arr. Mottl)				
Vienna Philharmonic	(1962)	[G] Elec E 80732	[G] Elec STE 80732	
		[E] ALP 1910	[E] ASD 478	
		[A] Ang 35746	[A] Ang S 35746	
GOTOVAC, JAKOV				
Ero der Schelm: Act 3 Kolo (Dance)				
Vienna Philharmonic	(1961)	[E] ALP 1930	[E] ASD 494	
		WRC T 763		
		[A] Ang 35975	[A] Ang S 35975	

Composer / Work / Collaborating Artists		Mono Recordings	Stereo / Quad Recordings	Cassettes
GOUNOD, CHARLES				
Faust: Waltz				
Vienna Philharmonic	(1961)	[E] ALP 1974	[E] ASD 525	
GRIEG, EDVARD				
Piano Concerto in A Minor, Op. 16				

Munich Philharmonic; Nelson Freire, pf.	(1968)		[G] CBS S 72712
			[E] CBS SPR 24
			    EMB 31041
			    CBS 61697
			[A] Col MS 7396
			    in Col M2X-798	

HANDEL, GEORGE FREDERICK				
Music for the Royal Fireworks				
Bamberg Symphony	(1962)	[G] Elec E 70495	[G] Elec STE 70495 Elec SME 70495	
HAYDN, FRANZ JOSEPH				
Symphony No. 93 in D				
Munich Philharmonic	(1969)		[G] DaCa Magna SM 91509	
Symphony No. 104 in D				
Philharmonia	(1956)	[G] Elec E 80454 [E] ALP 1471 MFP 2082 [A] Cap G 7150	[A] Cap SG 7150	
HEUBERGER, RICHARD				
Der Opernball: Overture				
Vienna Philharmonic	(1958)	[G] Elec E 80455	[G] Elec STE 80455 1C 151-01 463/64	[G] 4X2G-6109
		[E] ALP 1637	[E] ASD 279 SXLP 30083	
		[A] Cap G 7167	[A] Cap SG 7167 Sera SIB 6109	
HUMPERDINCK, ENGELBERT				
Hansel and Gretel: Suite (arr. Kempe)				
Royal Philharmonic	(1961)	[E] ALP 1892 WRC T 736	[E] ASD 460	
			[A] Sera S 60056	
JANACEK, LEOS				
Glagolitic Mass				
Royal Philharmonic; Teresa Kubiak, Anne Collins, Robert Tear, Wolfgang Schöne; Brighton Festival Chorus	(1973)		[G] Dec 6.42254 AW [E] Dec SXL 6600 [A] Lon OS 26338	[E] KSXC 6600
KHATCHATURIAN, ARAM				
Concerto for 'Cello and Orchestra				
Leipzig Radio Symphony; Wilhelm Posegga, vc.	(c. 1952)	[A] Urania 7119		
KODALY, ZOLTAN				
Hary Janos Suite, Op. 15				
Vienna Philharmonic	(1961)	[G] Elec E 70511 [E] ALP 1930 WRC T 763 [A] Ang 35975	[E] ASD 494 [A] Ang S 35975	

Composer / Work / Collaborating Artists		Mono Recordings	Stereo / Quad Recordings	Cassettes
KORNGOLD, ERICH				
Symphony in F-Sharp, Op. 40				
Munich Philharmonic	(1972)		[G] RCA 26.41 227AW	
			[E] RCA ARL 1-0443	[E] ARK 1-0443
			[A] RCA ARL 1-0443	
LEHAR, FRANZ				
Gold and Silver Waltz				
1. Vienna Philharmonic	(1958)	[G] Elec E 80455	[G] Elec STE 80455	
			1C 151-01 463/64	[G] 4X2G-6109
		[E] ALP 1637	[E] ASD 279	
		XLP 30060	SXLP 30060	
		[A] Cap G 7167	[A] Cap SG 7167	
			Sera SIB 6109	
2. Staatskapelle Dresden	(1972/73)		[G] Euro 86847 IU	[G] 55526 DU
			[E] RCA LRL 1-5044	
LISZT, FRANZ				
Totentanz				
Munich Philharmonic; Nelson Freire, pf.	(1968)		[G] CBS S 72713	
			[A] in Col M2X-798	
MAHLER, GUSTAV				
Kindertotenlieder				
Berlin Philharmonic; Dietrich Fischer-Dieskau, bar.	(1955)	[G] Elec E 70004	[G] Elec SME 91387 (r)	
			1C 063-00 898 (r)	
		[E] BLP 1081		
		XLP 30044		
		[A] Sera 60272		
MASCAGNI, PIETRO				
L'Amico Fritz: Intermezzo				
Vienna Philharmonic	(1961)	[E] ALP 1974	[E] ASD 525	
MENDELSSOHN, FELIX				
A Midsummer Night's Dream: *Overture, Nocturne, Scherzo, Wedding March*				
Royal Philharmonic	(1961)	[E] ALP 1892	[E] ASD 460	
		WRC T 736		
			[A] Sera S 60056	
Hebrides Overture, Op. 26				
Vienna Philharmonic	(1958)		[G] Kr. SMVP 8061	
		[E] ALP 1765	[E] ASD 330	
		XLP 30077	SXLP 30077	
Symphony No. 3 in A Minor, Op. 56				
Staatskapelle Dresden	(1951)	Ultra 23953/57		
		Supra LPM 11-12		
		[E] Parl PLP 142		
		[A] Parl PLP 142		
MOZART, WOLFGANG AMADEUS				
Four Concertos for Horn, K. 412 in D, and K. 417, 447, & 495 in E-Flat				
Royal Philharmonic; Alan Civil, horn	(1966)		[G] RCA LSC 2973-B	
		[E] WRC T 628	[E] WRC ST 628	[E] ZCWR 628
		[A] RCA LM 2973	[A] RCA LSC 2973	
Concerto Rondo for Horn in E-Flat, K. 371				
Royal Philharmonic; Alan Civil, horn	(1966)		[G] RCA LSC 2973-B	
		[E] WRC T 628	[E] WRC ST 628	[E] ZCWR 628
		[A] RCA LM 2973	[A] RCA LSC 2973	

Composer / Work / Collaborating Artists	Mono Recordings	Stereo / Quad Recordings	Cassettes
MOZART, WOLFGANG AMADEUS (cont.)			
Piano Concerto No. 27 in B-Flat, K. 595			
Munich Philharmonic; Friedrich Gulda, pf.	(1972)	[G] in BASF 29 21770-1 in MPS 88009	
Mass No. 19 in D Minor, K. 626 (Requiem)			
Berlin Philharmonic; Elisabeth Grümmer, Marga Höffgen, Helmut Krebs, Gottlob Frick; St Hedwig's Cathedral Choir	(1955) [G] Elec E 80006 1C 047-00 128 [E] ALP 1444 [A] Cap G 7113	[A] Pick 4039 (r)	
Overtures			
Cosi Fan Tutte			
Philharmonia	(1955) [G] Elec E 70045 [E] BLP 1088		
Idomeneo			
Philharmonia	(1955) [E] HMV 45 rpm 7ER 5074		
Magic Flute			
Philharmonia	(1955) [G] Elec E 70045 [E] BLP 1088 HMV 45 rpm 7ER 5074		
Marriage of Figaro			
Philharmonia	(1955) [G] Elec E 70045 [E] BLP 1088		
Serenade No. 13 in G, K. 525			
1. Philharmonia	(1955) [G] Elec E 70045 [E] BLP 1088		
2. Bamberg Symphony	(1963) [G] Euro 70654 KK	[G] Euro S 70655 KK Euro 85254 ZK Euro 27642 XAK	
	[E] Oriole RM 176 Oriole RM 202 Oriole RM 52202 WRC T 437		
Symphony No. 34 in C, K. 338			
Philharmonia	(1955) [G] Elec E 80454 [E] ALP 1471 MFP 2082 [A] Cap G 7150	[A] Cap SG 7150	
NICOLAI, OTTO			
Merry Wives of Windsor: Overture			
Vienna Philharmonic	(1958) [E] ALP 1765 XLP 30077	[G] Kr. SMVP 8061 [E] ASD 330 SXLP 30077	
OFFENBACH, JACQUES			
Orpheus in the Underworld: Overture			
Vienna Philharmonic	(1960) [E] ALP 1974 XLP 30077	[E] ASD 525 SXLP 30077	
PONCHIELLI, AMILCARE			
La Gioconda: Dance of the Hours			
Vienna Philharmonic	(1961) [E] ALP 1974	[E] ASD 525	
RESPIGHI, OTTORINO			
Pines of Rome			
Royal Philharmonic	(1964)	[A] RD 4-15-1 Quint. PMC 7005	

Composer / Work / Collaborating Artists		Mono Recordings	Stereo / Quad Recordings	Cassettes
REZNICEK, EMIL NIKOLAUS VON				
Donna Diana: Overture				
Vienna Philharmonic	(1958)	[G] Elec E 80455	[G] Elec STE 80455	
			1C 151-01 463/64	[G] 4X2G-6109
		[E] ALP 1637	[E] ASD 279	
		XLP 30060	SXLP 30060	
		[A] Cap G 7167	[A] Cap SG 7167	
			Sera SIB 6109	
RIMSKY-KORSAKOV, NIKOLAI				
Scheherazade, Op. 35				
Royal Philharmonic	(1967)		[E] WRC ST 657	
			CFP 174	
SCHMIDT, FRANZ				
Notre Dame: Intermezzo				
Vienna Philharmonic	(1961)	[E] ALP 1974	[E] ASD 525	
SCHOECK, OTHMAR				
Cantata: 'Vom Fischer un syner Fru'				
Munich Philharmonic; Karl Lövacs,	(1975)		[G] Acanta EA 22823	
Horst Laubenthal, Sigmund				
Nimsgern				
SCHUBERT, FRANZ				
Rosamunde: Incidental Music, D. 797				
Vienna Philharmonic	(1961)	[G] Elec E 80732	[G] Elec STE 80732	
		[E] ALP 1910	[E] ASD 478	
		[A] Ang 35746	[A] Ang S 35746	
Symphony No. 8 in B Minor, D. 759				
Bamberg Symphony	(1963)	[G] Euro 70470 KK	[G] Euro S 70471 KK	
			Euro 27642 XAK	
			in Euro 25490 XFK	
		[E] Oriole RM 201		
		Oriole RM 52201		
		WRC T 437		
Symphony No. 9 in C, D. 944				
Munich Philharmonic	(1968)		[G] CBS S 72710	
			[E] in CBS 78210	
SCHUMANN, ROBERT				
Piano Concerto in A Minor, Op. 54				
Munich Philharmonic; Nelson Freire,	(1968)		[G] CBS S 72713	
pf.			[A] in Col M2X-798	
Manfred: Overture, Op. 115				
Berlin Philharmonic	(1956)	[G] Elec E 60094		
		[E] ALP 1581		
		[A] Cap G 7117		
Symphony No. 1 in B-Flat, Op. 38				
Berlin Philharmonic	(1955)	[G] Elec E 70005		
		[E] ALP 1581		
		[A] Cap G 7117		
SMETANA, BEDRICH				
The Bartered Bride (Prodana Nevesta)				
Complete; Sung in German				
Bamberg Symphony; RIAS Chamber	(1962)	[G] Elec E 91226/27	[G] Elec STE 91226/27	
Choir		and E 91228S	and STE 91228S	
Cast: Pilar Lorengar, Fritz			1C 153-28 922/93	

Composer / Work / Collaborating Artists		Mono Recordings	Stereo / Quad Recordings	Cassettes
SMETANA, BEDRICH (cont.)				
	Wunderlich, Karl-Ernst Mercker, Gottlob Frick, Nada Puttar, Marcel Cordes, Sieglinde Wagner, Ivan Sardi, Ernst Krukowski, Walter Stoll	[E] ALPS 1971 and ALP 1972/73 [A] Ang 3642C	[E] ASDS 522 and ASD 523/24 HQS 1132/34 [A] Ang S 3642C	
	> Highlights of the above:	[G] Elec E 80746	[G] Elec STE 80746 Elec SME 80746 1C 063-29 002	[G] 89 501
The Bartered Bride: Orchestral Selections i. Overture, ii. Polka, iii. Furiant, iv. Dance of the Comedians				
1.	Vienna Philharmonic (i. only)	(1958) [E] ALP 1765 XLP 30077	[G] Kr. SMVP 8061 [E] ASD 330 SXLP 30077	
2.	Royal Philharmonic (i, ii, iii, iv)	(1961) [E] ALP 1880	[E] ASD 449 SXLP 30125 [A] Sera S 60098	
The Bartered Bride: Aria: 'Endlich allein' (Sung in German)				
	Berlin Philharmonic; Elisabeth Lindermeier, s.	(1957) [G] Elec E 80027		
Ma Vlast: 'From Bohemia's Woods and Fields'				
	Bamberg Symphony	(1963) [G] Euro 70654 KK [E] Oriole RM 202 Oriole RM 52202 WRC T 424	[G] Euro S 70655 KK	
STRAUSS, JOHANN, I Radetzky March				
	Vienna Philharmonic	(1958) [G] Elec E 80455 [E] ALP 1637 XLP 30060 [A] Cap G 7167	[G] Elec STE 80455 1C 151-01 463/64 [E] ASD 279 SXLP 30060 [A] Cap SG 7167 Sera SIB 6109	[G] 4X2G-6109
STRAUSS, JOHANN, II Die Fledermaus: Overture				
1.	Vienna Philharmonic	(1958) [G] Elec E 80455 [E] ALP 1637 [A] Cap G 7167	[G] Elec STE 80455 1C 151-01 463/64 [E] ASD 279 SXLP 30083 [A] Cap SG 7167 Sera SIB 6109	[G] 4X2G-6109
2.	Staatskapelle Dresden	(1972/73)	[G] Euro 86847 IU [E] RCA LRL 1-5044	[G] 55526 DU
Emperor Waltz				
	Vienna Philharmonic	(1960) [E] ALP 1861 [A] Ang 35851	[G] 1C 151-01 463/64 [E] ASD 431 SXLP 30083 [A] Ang S 35851 Sera SIB 6109	[G] 4X2G-6109

Composer / Work / Collaborating Artists		Mono Recordings	Stereo / Quad Recordings	Cassettes
Im Krapfenwald'l Polka				
Vienna Philharmonic	(1960)		[G] 1C 151-01 463/64	[G] 4X2G-6109
		[E] ALP 1861	[E] ASD 431	
			SXLP 30083	
		[A] Ang 35851	[A] Ang S 35851	
			Sera SIB 6109	
Leichtes Blut Polka				
1. Vienna Philharmonic	(1960)		[G] 1C 151-01 463/64	[G] 4X2G-6109
		[E] ALP 1861	[E] ASD 431	
		XLP 30060	SXLP 30060	
		[A] Ang 35851	[A] Ang S 35851	
			Sera SIB 6109	
2. Staatskapelle Dresden	(1972/73)		[G] Euro 86847 IU	[G] 55526 DU
			[E] RCA LRL 1-5044	
Tales of the Vienna Woods				
1. Vienna Philharmonic	(1960)		[G] 1C 151-01 463/64	[G] 4X2G-6109
		[E] ALP 1861	[E] ASD 431	
		XLP 30060	SXLP 30060	
		[A] Ang 35851	[A] Ang S 35851	
			Sera SIB 6109	
2. Staatskapelle Dresden	(1972/73)		[G] Euro 86847 IU	[G] 55526 DU
			[E] RCA LRL 1-5044	
Thousand and One Nights: Intermezzo				
Vienna Philharmonic	(1960)		[G] 1C 151-01 463/64	[G] 4X2G-6109
		[E] ALP 1861	[E] ASD 431	
			SXLP 30083	
		[A] Ang 35851	[A] Ang S 35851	
			Sera SIB 6109	
STRAUSS, JOSEPH				
Dynamiden Waltz				
Vienna Philharmonic	(1958)		[G] 1C 151-01 463/64	[G] 4X2G-6109
		[E] ALP 1861	[E] ASD 431	
			SXLP 30083	
		[A] Ang 35851	[A] Ang S 35851	
			Sera SIB 6109	
Sphärenklänge Waltz				
1. Vienna Philharmonic	(1958)	[G] Elec E 80455	[G] Elec STE 80455	
			1C 151-01 463/64	[G] 4X2G-6109
		[E] ALP 1637	[E] ASD 279	
		XLP 30060	SXLP 30060	
		[A] Cap G 7167	[A] Cap SG 7167	
			Sera SIB 6109	
2. Staatskapelle Dresden	(1972/73)		[G] Euro 86847 IU	[G] 55526 DU
			[E] RCA LRL 1-5044	
STRAUSS, RICHARD				
Burleske for Piano & Orch. in D Minor				
Staatskapelle Dresden; Malcolm Frager, pf.	(1975)		[G] in 1C 191-02 743/46(Q)	
			1C 063-02 744(Q)	[G] 1C 263-02 744
			[E] in SLS 5067(Q)	[E] TC SLS 5067
			ASD 3399(Q)	TC ASD 3399
			[A] Ang S 32767(Q)	
Concertino for Clarinet, Bassoon, Harp, and Strings				
Staatskapelle Dresden; Manfred Weise, Wolfgang Liebscher	(1975)		[G] in 1C 191-02 743/46(Q)	
			[E] in SLS 5067(Q)	[E] TC SLS 5067

Composer / Work / Collaborating Artists	Mono Recordings	Stereo / Quad Recordings	Cassettes
STRAUSS, RICHARD *(cont.)*			
Concerto for Horn No. 1 in E-Flat, Op. 11			
1. Royal Philharmonic; Alan Civil, horn	(1967)	[A] RD 4-60-1	
2. Staatskapelle Dresden; Peter Damm, horn	(1975)	[G] in 1C 191-02 743/46(Q) 1C 063-02 743(Q) [E] in SLS 5067(Q) [A] Ang S 37004(Q)	[G] 1C 243-02 743 [E] TC SLS 5067
Concerto for Horn No. 2 in E-Flat			
Staatskapelle Dresden; Peter Damm, horn	(1975)	[G] in 1C 191-02 743/46(Q) 1C 063-02 743(Q) [E] in SLS 5067(Q) [A] Ang S 37004(Q)	[G] 1C 243-02 743 [E] TC SLS 5067
Concerto for Oboe in D			
Staatskapelle Dresden; Manfred Clement, oboe	(1975)	[G] in 1C 191-02 743/46(Q) [E] in SLS 5067(Q) ESD 7026	[E] TC SLS 5067 TC ESD 7026
Concerto for Violin in D Minor, Op. 8			
Staatskapelle Dresden; Ulf Hoelscher, v.	(1975)	[G] in 1C 191-02 743/46(Q) 1C 063-02 744(Q) [E] in SLS 5067(Q) ASD 3399(Q) [A] Ang S 3267(Q)	[G] 1C 263-02 744 [E] TC SLS 5067 TC ASD 3399
Panathenaenzug for Piano, Op. 74			
Staatskapelle Dresden; Peter Rösel, pf.	(1975)	[G] in 1C 191-02 743/46(Q) [E] in SLS 5067(Q)	[E] TC SLS 5067
Parergon zu Sinfonia Domestica, Op. 73			
Staatskapelle Dresden; Peter Rösel, pf.	(1975)	[G] in 1C 191-02 743/46(Q) [E] in SLS 5067(Q)	[E] TC SLS 5067
Ariadne auf Naxos, Op. 60 (Complete)			
Staatskapelle Dresden *Cast:* Hermann Prey, Wilfried Schaal, Peter Schreier, Teresa Zylis-Gara, James King, Günter Dressler, Sylvia Geszty, Gundula Janowitz, Erika Wüstmann, Adele Stolte, Annelies Burmeister, Siegfried Vogel, Theo Adam, Hans-Joachim Rotzsch, Erich Alexander Winds	(1968)	[G] Ang SMA 91 771/73 1C 165-00 110/12 [E] Ang SAN 215/17 SLS 936	
> *Highlights of the above:*		[G] 1C 063-00 824	
Capriccio: Moonlight Music			
Staatskapelle Dresden	(1970/71)	[G] Eterna 826 439 (East Germany)	
Der Rosenkavalier, Op. 59 (Complete)			
Staatskapelle Dresden and Opera Chorus *Cast:* Margarete Baumer, Kurt Böhme, Tiana Lemnitz, Hans Lobel, Ursula Richter, Angela Kolniak, Franz Sautter, Emilie Walther-Sacks	(1950) [G] Acanta JA 23039 [E] Nixa ULP 9201 1/4 [A] Urania 201	[A] Urania 5201-4 (r)	
> *Highlights of the above:*	[E] Nixa ULP 9026 [A] Urania 7062		
> *Preludes to Acts I and III*	[E] Saga XID 5117 in Nixa ULP 9602 1/2 [A] in Urania 602 in Urania 8010	[A] in Urania 58010 (r)	

Composer / Work / Collaborating Artists	Mono Recordings	Stereo / Quad Recordings	Cassettes
Der Rosenkavalier: Waltzes			
Staatskapelle Dresden	(1971/73)	[G] in 1C 195-50 344/46	
		[E] in SLS 880	
		ASD 3074	
		[A] Ang S 37046	
Salome: Dance of the 7 Veils			
Staatskapelle Dresden	(1970)	[G] in 1C 195-52 100/02	
		1C 063-02 344	[G] 1C 263-02 344
		1C 037-03 255	1C 7300 280
		[E] in SLS 894	[E] in TC SLS 899
		ESD 7026	TC ESD 7026
		[A] Sera S 60297(Q)	[A] 4XG-60297
Schlagobers: Waltz			
Staatskapelle Dresden	(1970/71)	[G] in 1C 191-50 271/74	
		[E] in SLS 861	
Alpine Symphony, Op. 64			
1. Royal Philharmonic	(1966)	[G] RCA 26.41 092AW	
	[E] RCA RB 6696	[E] RCA SB 6696	
	[A] RCA LM 2923	[A] RCA LSC 2923	
2. Staatskapelle Dresden	(1971)	[G] in 1C 191-50 271/74	
		1C 063-02 341(Q)	[G] 1C 243-02 341
		[E] in SLS 861	
		ASD 3173	[E] TC ASD 3173
Also sprach Zarathustra, Op. 30			
Staatskapelle Dresden	(1971)	[G] in 1C 191-50 271/74	
		1C 063-02 342(Q)	[G] 1C 243-02 342
		[E] in SLS 861	[E] in TC SLS 899
		ESD 7026	TC ESD 7026
		[A] Sera S 60283(Q)	[A] 4XG-60283
Aus Italien, Op. 16			
Staatskapelle Dresden	(1972/74)	[G] in 1C 195-52 100/02	
		1C 063-02 533(Q)	[G] 1C 243-02 533
		[E] in SLS 894	
		ASD 3319	[E] TC ASD 3319
		[A] Sera S 60301(Q)	
Le Bourgeois Gentilhomme Suite, Op. 60			
Staatskapelle Dresden	(1970/71)	[G] in 1C 191-50 271/74	
		[E] in SLS 861	
Don Juan, Op. 20			
1. Royal Philharmonic	(1964)	[A] RD 4-15-1	
		Quint. PMC 7005	
2. Staatskapelle Dresden	(1970/71)	[G] in 1C 191-50 271/74	
		1C 063-02 342(Q)	[G] 1C 243-02 342
		[E] in SLS 861	[E] in TC SLS 899
		[A] Sera S 60288(Q)	
Don Quixote, Op. 35			
1. Berlin Philharmonic; Paul Tortelier, vc.	(1958) [G] Elec E 80438	[G] Elec STE 80438	
		1C 037-03 255	[G] 7300 280
	[E] ALP 1759	[E] ASD 326	
	WRC T 609	WRC ST 609	
	[A] Cap G 7190	[A] Cap SG 7190	
		Sera S 60122	
2. Staatskapelle Dresden; Paul Tortelier, vc.	(1970/73)	[G] in 1C 195-50 344/46	
		[E] in SLS 880	
		ASD 3074	
		[A] Ang S 37046	

Composer / Work / Collaborating Artists	Mono Recordings	Stereo / Quad Recordings	Cassettes
STRAUSS, RICHARD (cont.)			
Ein Heldenleben, Op. 40			
Staatskapelle Dresden	(1971/72)	[G] in 1C 195-50 344/46	
		[E] in SLS 880	[E] in TC SLS 899
		[A] Sera S 60315(Q)	[A] 4XG-60315
Josephslegende			
Staatskapelle Dresden	(1973/74)	[G] in 1C 195-52 100/02	
		[E] in SLS 894	
Macbeth, Op. 23			
Staatskapelle Dresden	(1970/71)	[G] in 1C 191-50 271/74	
		[E] in SLS 861	
		[A] Sera S 60288(Q)	
Metamorphosen for 23 Solo Strings			
1. Munich Philharmonic	(1968)	[G] CBS S 72711	
2. Staatskapelle Dresden	(1970/71)	[G] in 1C 191-50 271/74	
		[E] in SLS 861	
Sinfonia Domestica, Op. 53			
Staatskapelle Dresden	(1972)	[G] in 1C 195-52 100/02	
		[E] in SLS 894	
Suite: Harpsichord Pieces by Couperin			
Staatskapelle Dresden	(1970/73)	[G] in 1C 195-50 344/46	
		[E] in SLS 880	
Till Eulenspiegel, Op. 28			
1. Berlin Philharmonic	(1958) [G] Elec E 80438	[G] Elec STE 80438	
	[E] ALP 1759	[E] ASD 326	
	WRC T 609	WRC ST 609	
	[A] Cap G 7190	[A] Cap SG 7190	
		Sera S 60122	[A] 4XG-60297
2. Staatskapelle Dresden	(1970)	[G] in 1C 195-52 100/02	
		1C 063-02 344	[G] 1C 263-02 344
		[E] in SLS 894	[E] in TC SLS 899
		ESD 7026	TC ESD 7026
		[A] Sera S 60297(Q)	
Tod und Verklärung, Op. 24			
Staatskapelle Dresden	(1970/71)	[G] in 1C 195-50 344/46	
		1C 063-02 344	[G] 1C 263-02 344
		[E] in SLS 880	
		[A] Sera S 60297(Q)	
STRAVINSKY, IGOR			
Firebird Suite			
Staatskapelle Dresden	(1976)	[G] Eterna 827 012	
		(East Germany)	
SUPPE, FRANZ VON			
Morning, Noon and Night Overture			
1. Vienna Philharmonic	(1958) [G] Elec E 80455	[G] Elec STE 80455	
		1C 151-01 463/64	[G] 4X2G-6109
	[E] ALP 1637	[E] ASD 279	
	XLP 30060	SXLP 30060	
	[A] Cap G 7167	[A] Cap SG 7167	
		Sera SIB 6109	
2. Staatskapelle Dresden	(1972/73)	[G] Euro 86847 IU	[G] 55526 DU
		[E] RCA LRL 1-5044	

Composer / Work / Collaborating Artists	Mono Recordings	Stereo / Quad Recordings	Cassettes
TCHAIKOVSKY, PETER ILYITCH			
Piano Concerto No. 1 in B-Flat Minor, Op. 23			

Munich Philharmonic; Nelson Freire, pf.	(1968)	[G] CBS S 72712
		[E] CBS SPR 24
		   in CBS 78210
		   EMB 31041
		   CBS 61697
		[A] Col MS 7396
		   in Col M2X 798
			[E] CBS 40 61697

Eugene Onegin: Selections—*i. Letter Scene; ii. Polonaise; iii. Act II Waltz; iv. 'Welch Festesglanz'* (sung in German)			
Berlin Philharmonic; Elisabeth Lindermeier, s.; Chorus of Berlin City Opera	(1957) [G] Elec E 80027 Elec E 80440		
> *ii. Polonaise only*		[G] in 1C 151-30 641/42 (r)	[G] 1C 227-30 641/42
Suite No. 3 in G, Op. 55: Theme & Variations			
Vienna Philharmonic	(1961) [E] ALP 1930 WRC T 763 [A] Ang 35975	[E] ASD 494 [A] Ang S 35975	
Symphony No. 5 in E Minor, Op. 64			

Berlin Philharmonic	(1959)
	[E] ALP 1800
	
	[A] Cap G 7219
		[G] Elec STE 80509
		[E] ASD 379
		   WRC ST 673
		   SXLP 30216
		[A] Cap SG 7219
			[E] TC SXLP 30216

Symphony No. 6 in B Minor, Op. 74			
Philharmonia	(1957) [E] ALP 1566 [A] Cap G 7128		
WAGNER, RICHARD			
Lohengrin (complete)			

1. Bavarian State Opera and Chorus
   Cast: George Vincent, Marianne Schech, Andreas Boehm, Margarete Klose, Kurt Böhme, Willi Wolff
	(1952) [G] BASF 40 223264
	   Acanta HB 22326
	[E] Nixa ULP 9225 1/5
	[A] Urania 225		

> *Highlights of the above:*	[G] Vox OPL 110 [E] Vox OPL 110 [A] Urania 7123 Vox PL 15.150	[A] Vox STPL 515.150 (r)	
> *Preludes to Acts I and III*	[E] Saga XID 5117 [A] Urania 7077 in Urania 8010	[A] in Urania 58010 (r)	

2. Vienna Philharmonic and Chorus of Vienna State Opera
   Cast: Jess Thomas, Elisabeth Grümmer, Dietrich Fischer-Dieskau, Christa Ludwig, Gottlob Frick, Otto Wiener
	(1962/63)
	
	[E] Ang AN 121/25
	
	[A] Ang 3641 E/L
		[G] Elec STA 91 299/03
		   1C 161-00 017/21
		[E] Ang SAN 121/25
		   SLS 5071
		[A] Ang S 3641 E/L
			[E] TC SLS 5071

> *Highlights of the above:*		[G] Elec SME 80853 1C 063-00 747	

Composer / Work / Collaborating Artists		Mono Recordings	Stereo / Quad Recordings	Cassettes
WAGNER, RICHARD (*cont.*)				
Lohengrin: Preludes to Acts I and III				
Vienna Philharmonic	(1958)	[G] Elec E 80456		
		[E] ALP 1638		
		XLP 30048		
		[A] Cap G 7180	[A] Cap SG 7180	
Die Meistersinger (complete)				
1. Staatskapelle Dresden and Opera Chorus	(1951)	[A] Urania 206		
Cast: Ferdinand Frantz, Kurt Böhme, Johannes Kemter, Kurt Legner, Heinrich Pflanzl, Karl Paul, Karl-Heinz Thomann, Heinrich Tessmer, Gerhard Stolze, Theo Adam, Erich Händel, Werner Faulhaber, Bernd Aldenhoff, Gerhard Unger, Tiana Lemnitz, Emilie Walther-Sacks, Werner Faulhaber		Vox OPBX 142		
> *Highlights of the above:*		>[G] Vox OPL 350		
		BASF 22 292673		
		Acanta DE 29267		
		[E] Vox OPL 350		
		[A] Urania 7067		
		Vox OPL 350		
		Vox PL 15.100	[A] Vox STPL 515.100 (r)	
> *Miscellaneous excerpts:*		>[E] Saga XID 5117		
		Saga XID 5290	[E] Saga ST XID 5290 (r)	
		[A] Urania 7077		
		in Urania 8010	[A] in Urania 58010 (r)	
2. Berlin Philharmonic and St Hedwig's Cathedral Choir and Chorus of the Municipal Opera and German State Opera Berlin	(1956)	[G] Elec E 90008/12		
		[E] ALP 1506/10		
		HQM 1094/98		
		[A] Ang 3572 E/L		
Cast: Ferdinand Frantz, Gottlob Frick, Horst Wilhelm, Walter Stoll, Benno Kusche, Gustav Neidlinger, Manfred Schmidt, Leopold Clam, Herold Kraus, Robert Koffmane, Anton Metternich, Hanns Pick, Rudolf Schock, Gerhard Unger, Elisabeth Grümmer, Marga Höffgen, Hermann Prey				
> *Highlights of 2nd recording:*			>[G] Elec SME 80923 (r)	
		[E] ALP 2253	1C 063-00 746 (r)	
> *Preludes to Acts I and III:*		>[G] Elec E 60094		
Die Meistersinger: Prelude to Act I				
Munich Philharmonic	(1972)		[G] in BASF 29 21770-1	
			in MPS 88009	
Das Rheingold: Highlights—*i. In the depths of the Rhine; ii. Transformation music to Scene 4; iii. Alberich's Curse; iv. Erde's Warning; v. Entrance of the Gods to Valhalla*				
German State Opera Berlin	(1959)	[G] Elec E 80470	[G] Elec STE 80470	
Cast: Ferdinand Frantz, Johanna Blatter, Benno Kusche, Helmut Melchert, Josef Metternich, Rudolf Schock, Ruth Siewert, Lisa Otto, Melitta Muszely, Sieglinde Wagner		[E] ALP 1984	[E] ASD 535	
			CFP 109	

Composer/Work/Collaborating Artists	Mono Recordings	Stereo/Quad Recordings	Cassettes

The Flying Dutchman: Overture
   Berlin Philharmonic (1956) [G] Elec E 80016
                                                    [E] ALP 1513
                                                        XLP 30040
                                                  [A] Ang 35574

Die Götterdämmerung: Dawn and
   Siegfried's Rhine Journey
   Berlin Philharmonic (1956) [G] Elec E 80016
                                                   [E] ALP 1513
                                                     XLP 30040
                                                 [A] Ang 35574

Parsifal: Prelude and Good Friday Music
   Vienna Philharmonic (1958) [G] Elec E 80456
                                               [E] ALP 1638
                                                   XLP 30048
                                              [A] Cap G 7180   [A] Cap SG 7180

Tannhäuser: Overture and Venusberg
   Music
   Berlin Philharmonic (1956) [G] Elec E 80016
                                               [E] ALP 1513
                                                   XLP 30040
                                               [A] Ang 35574

Tristan and Isolde: Prelude and
   Liebestod
   Vienna Philharmonic (1958) [G] Elec E 80456
                                               [E] ALP 1638
                                                   XLP 30048
                                              [A] Cap G 7180   [A] Cap SG 7180

WEBER, CARL MARIA VON
Der Freischütz ('complete'—dialogue cuts)
   Staatskapelle Dresden & Opera (1951) [G] BASF 22 292268-1
   Chorus   Acanta DE 29268
   Cast: Karl Paul, Werner Faulhaber,   [A] Urania 403
   Elfriede Trötschel, Irma Beilke, Kurt   Urania 242/3   [A] Urania 5242/3 (r)
   Böhme, Bernd Aldenhoff, Heinz   in Vox OPBX 149
   Kramer, Karl-Heinz Thomann,
   Hannes Haegle

> Highlights of the above: [G] Vox OPL 260
                                                   [E] Vox OPL 260

Euryanthe: Overture
   Bamberg Symphony (1963) [G] Euro 70654 KK   [G] Euro S 70655 KK   [G] in Euro 48204 UK
                                                                                in Euro 47400 NK   in Euro 56156 QK
                                                                                in Euro 87372 XBK
                                         [E] Oriole RM 202
                                                   Oriole RM 52202

Oberon: Overture
   Vienna Philharmonic (1958)   [G] Kr. SMVP 8061
                                       [E] ALP 1765   [E] ASD 330
                                             XLP 30077   SXLP 30077

WEINBERGER, JAROMIR
Schwanda the Bagpiper: Polka & Fugue
   Royal Philharmonic (1961) [E] ALP 1880   [E] ASD 449
                                                                         SXLP 30125
                                                                         [A] Sera S 60098

Acknowledgements

I would like to express my warmest thanks to Senator h.c. Günther Klinge for his generous support and advice which enabled the German edition of this book to be released in 1977. Dr. Jürgen Kolbe on behalf of the City of Munich has also contributed financial support. Furthermore I would like to thank Dr. Brian Large for his assistance in preparing the English version of the text, as well as Peter Cochrane and Christopher Foster of Springwood Books for their marvellous co-operation. Denham Ford and Charles Blyth thoroughly revised and enlarged the discography, and many others of our personal friends and musician colleagues, especially in this country, provided invaluable help and encouragement. Of them I am particularly grateful to Dietrich Fischer-Dieskau, Romi Freund, Dr. Jeffrey Tate and Anneliese Riedl, to Archie Newman, David Sigall, Susan Alcock, Harry Legge, Frederick and Lotte Hoffman, my parents and—last but not least—to my friend and teacher, Max Rostal.

Munich, February 1979   Cordula Kempe-Oettinger

Illustration Acknowledgements

Artricia, London pp. 148, 149
James Aurig, Dresden p. 37 No. 2
Clive Barda, London pp. 138, 139, 140
B.B.C., London p. 151
Studio Bernateau, Orange pp. 144 No. 2, 145 No. 2
Betz, Theatre Archive, Munich p. 52
Dr. Roger Botella, Paris p. 126
Donald Cooper, London pp. 130 Nos. 2 and 3, 131
Daily Telegraph, London p. 150 No. 1
Decca Recording, London p. 98
Electrola/Berger, Berlin p. 70
Electrola/Karnine p. 81
E.M.I./Huttar, Vienna p. 68 No. 1
Felici, Vatican, Rome p. 89
Gentbe, Leipzig p. 44

G.L.C., London p. 75 No. 1
The *Guardian*, London p. 150 No. 2
Elfriede Hanak, Vienna pp. 66 Nos. 2 and 3, 67 Nos. 1 and 3, 68 No. 2, 69
Klaus Hennch, Zurich pp. 85 No. 2, 86, 87, 133
G. Hoenisch, Leipzig p. 41
Hildegard Jaeckel, Dresden pp. 13, 49, 50
Willi Kasper, Seifhennersdorf p. 47 No. 1
Rudolf Kempe pp. 46 No. 1, 48 No. 2, 71, 85 No. 1, 88, 90
Cordula Kempe, Munich pp. 127, 130 No. 1, 145 No. 1
Keystone, London pp. 72 No. 1, 75 No. 2
Siegfried Lauterwasser, Uberlingen pp. 82 Nos. 3 and 4, 83, 132

Sedge Le Blanc, New York pp. 64, 65
Gerhard Lenssen, Munich p. 144 No. 1
A. Madner, Salzburg pp. 66 No. 1, 67 No. 2
Hansjoachim Mirschel, D.D.R. Berlin pp. 124, 125, 134, 135, 142, 143
Werner Neumeister, Munich pp. 48 No. 1, 95, 121, 122, 123, 128, 129, 136, 137, 156 Nos. 2 and 3, 157, 158, 159, 160
Gerard Noel, London p. 141
Lotte Oettinger, Stuttgart p. 156 No. 1
Press Association, London p. 78
Rauh, Bayreuth Festival pp. 82 Nos. 1, 2 and 5, 84
Evelyn Richter, Leipzig pp. 92, 93, 152, 153, 154, 155

Houston Rodgers, London pp. 63, 73 No. 1
Royal Philharmonic Orchestra, London pp. 76, 77, 79, 91
Dr. Ursula Rübsamen, Dresden p. 51 No. 1
Christine Stephan-Brosch, Karl-Marx-Stadt pp. 96, 97
Irmgard Steup, Schweinfurt p. 80
The Times, London p. 72 No. 2
Sabine Toepffer, Munich pp. 53, 54, 94
United Nations, New York pp. 99, 100
Varenholz, Dresden p. 51 No. 2
Harry Weber, Austria p. 74
Reg Wilson, London p. 73 No. 2
Unknown photographers pp. 37 Nos. 1 and 3, 38, 39, 40, 42, 43, 45, 46 No. 2, 47 No. 2, 51 No. 3, 146, 147